The dBASE Programming Language

M. de Pace

COLLINS
8 Grafton Street, London W1

Other books of interest

Working with dBase II
M. de Pace
0 00 383251 1

dBase III: A Practical Guide
M. de Pace
0 00 383076 4

MS/PC DOS Prompt
Randall McMullan
0 00 383288 0

Wordstar in Action
Randall McMullan
0 00 383107 8

Wordstar Prompt
Randall McMullan
0 246 12446 6

SuperCalc Prompt
Randall McMullan
0 00 383004 7

The Pick Operating System
Joseph St. John Bate and Ross Burgess
0 00 383160 4

The Automated Office
Joseph St. John Bate and Ross Burgess
0 00 383008 X

Office Automation Using the IBM Personal Computer Systems
Joseph St. John Bate and Ross Burgess
0 00 383104 3

Contents

Collins Professional and Technical Books
William Collins Sons & Co. Ltd
8 Grafton Street, London W1X 3LA

First published in Great Britain by
Collins Professional and Technical Books 1986

British Library Cataloguing in Publication Data
De Pace, M.
The dBASE programming language.
   1.   dBASE II (Computer program)
   2.   dBASE III (Computer program)
   I. Title
   005.74   QA76.9.D3

ISBN 0-00-383267-8

Photoset in North Wales by
Derek Doyle & Associates, Mold, Clwyd
Printed and bound in Great Britain by
Robert Hartnoll (1985) Ltd,
Bodmin, Cornwall

Preface

This book is concerned with the *dBASE language* and while it concentrates on the major implementations of the language such as dBASE II and dBASE III, it also draws attention to other implementations such as FoxBASE, dB Compiler, and the Clipper compiler. It is, however, more concerned with the specification and use of the language itself than with any one implementation.

There are two major specifications, that of dBASE II and that of dBASE III. The dBASE II specification has been implemented in dBASE II itself, in Wordtech's pseudo compiler called dB Compiler, and in Fox Software's FoxBASE. The latter is of particular interest since it also offers a Unix and Xenix implementation of the dBASE II specification. The dBASE III specification has so far been implemented successfully in dBASE III, dBASE III PLUS, and the Clipper compiler. Fox Software have announced a fully compatible dBASE III PLUS look-alike, but at the time of writing it has not yet arrived. When it does, and if it has a Unix and Xenix implementation, it will of course be of tremendous interest.

Because this book is concerned with the dBASE language, particular attention has been paid to those implementations which have taken the language to its highest level so far, as found in dBASE III PLUS and the Clipper compiler. However, the dBASE II specification seen in dBASE II itself and in totally compatible products like FoxBASE, is comprehensively covered to satisfy the needs of the very large number of dBASE II users and because it represents the original specification of the dBASE language. Another point which arises from the fact that we are here concerned with dBASE as a programming language, is that you will find little coverage of commands that would not have a place in a program, for example a purely interactive command such as ASSIST.

Ashton Tate, who gave birth to the dBASE language, will continue to play an important role, but they are no longer the only players in this field. The dBASE language has become so popular that Ashton Tate's grip on their child has been loosened: the child has outgrown the parent. dBASE has become a standard programming language, and both compiler writers and interpreter writers have created products which have enhanced the status of the dBASE language. In response Ashton Tate are themselves continually refining and improving their interpreter.

The dBASE language has already earned the epithet of fourth generation language from several industry commentators and, before long, it should be available on mainframe computers. It has already broken loose from its origins in the microcomputer fold to become available on minicomputers such as those supplied by DEC and Altos. It is now a fully fledged programming language which not only ranks favourably in comparison with other longer established computer languages, but represents a more natural introduction to computer programming than almost any other programming language.

If we are concerned with the need to develop computer skills, then we can do no better than turn the attention of our students to a language that can be assimilated in hours rather than weeks, and which can lead to productive use within days rather than months. And because it is a structured language, it teaches good programming habits rather than bad ones, so that a dBASE programmer will find it much easier to find employment in a corporate environment than would a BASIC programmer.

The really nice thing about dBASE is that you become a convert to it almost as soon as you have seen it in operation. For example, if you remain unconvinced regarding the claimed advantages of dBASE as a language as opposed to those of more traditional languages such as COBOL, you need only turn to page 4 for a comparison: the COBOL program requires 57 lines of program code; the equivalent dBASE program needs only 3 lines.

I would encourage teachers and students to turn from traditional programming languages to dBASE much as one would encourage a farmer to use a combine harvester instead of a scythe. The capital investment required to teach dBASE is so much less as well: it needs only an inexpensive microcomputer. With the price of equipment falling year after year, students could these days afford to teach themselves at home.

As a final point, the mystique that surrounds computers and programming has fortunately begun to disperse, and people are now realising that it is as easy to drive a computer as it is to drive a car or a motorbike. With the dBASE programming language the difference is that you find yourself able to drive usefully during your very first lesson.

M. de Pace

Chapter One
Introducing the dBASE Programming Language

The dBASE programming language began life as an extra feature to a database product for microcomputers called dBASE II. The product was essentially an attempt to duplicate the database facilities available on large computers whereby computer programmers were spared the need to provide programs for basic information handling functions such as finding a required item of information. Instead the database software was preprogrammed to perform a large number of standard tasks so that the programmer simply had to tell the database software what to do next. The programmers still had to take care of issues such as performing calculations, or deciding which items to group together, or dealing with the precise appearance of a printed document, but there was no need to concern themselves with the technical detail of finding bits of data in a computer file. The situation was akin to being able to drive a car without needing to know how the engine works.

The dBASE II software received its instructions from the microcomputer user by means of commands such as LIST or SUM. The software displayed a prompt (a signal to the user to use the keyboard to enter information) and then waited for the user to enter one of a predefined set of commands. If the command was legitimate, the software would carry out the requested function. Thus a user might ask the software to LIST all items and when that had been accomplished, request that they be counted (COUNT) or totalled (SUM). Usually the commands would be extended by adding the names of data items held in the database file, for example SUM COST, and by adding conditions so that the command would apply only to selected records, for example SUM COST FOR CATEGORY = 1.

From these 'one at a time' commands it was a simple progression to the concept of allowing the user to store successive commands on a diskette so that dBASE II could attend to all the commands, one after the other, without requiring the intervention of the user. Thus dBASE programs were born, because a program is nothing more than a series of successive commands which can be executed by the computer without having recourse to the programmer.

Let us look at a simple dBASE program that reads through a stock file and writes to another file the stock levels for all stock items with a product code in the range 1001 to 2000:

```
use stock
copy to extract fields code,level for code > "1000" .and. code < "2001"
quit
```

The program reads a file called STOCK and creates a new file called EXTRACT, writing to it the product code and stock level of all products with a product code in the range 1001 to 2000. Now let us look at a COBOL program that performs exactly the same function:

```
000100 IDENTIFICATION DIVISION.
000200 PROGRAM-ID. COPY.
000300 ENVIRONMENT DIVISION.
000400 CONFIGURATION SECTION.
000500 SOURCE-COMPUTER.      IBM-PC.
000600 OBJECT-COMPUTER.      IBM-PC.
000700 INPUT-OUTPUT SECTION.
000800 FILE-CONTROL.
000900     SELECT MASTER-FILE ASSIGN TO "STOCK.DAT"
001000         ORGANIZATION IS SEQUENTIAL.
001100     SELECT COPY-FILE ASSIGN TO "EXTRACT.DAT"
001200         ORGANIZATION IS SEQUENTIAL.
001300 DATA DIVISION.
001400 FILE SECTION.
001500 FD  MASTER-FILE.
001600 01  M-REC.
001700     02  M-CODE        PIC X(5).
001800     02  M-DESC        PIC X(20).
001900     02  M-COST        PIC 999V99.
002000     02  M-LEVEL       PIC 9(6).
002100 FD  COPY-FILE.
002200 01  C-REC.
002300     02  C-CODE        PIC X(5).
002400     02  C-LEVEL       PIC 9(6).
002500 WORKING-STORAGE SECTION.
002600 77  RESULT            PIC 9(8)V99.
002700 PROCEDURE DIVISION.
002800 A-MAINLINE SECTION.
002900 A-10.
003000     PERFORM B-INIT.
003100     PERFORM C-MAIN.
```

```
003200      PERFORM D-END.
003300      STOP RUN.
003400 A-EXIT.
003500      EXIT.
003600 B-INIT SECTION.
003700 B-10.
003800      OPEN INPUT MASTER-FILE
003900           OUTPUT COPY-FILE.
004100 B-EXIT.
004200      EXIT.
004300 C-MAIN SECTION.
004400 C-10.
004500      READ MASTER-FILE AT END GO TO C-EXIT.
004600      IF M-CODE GREATER THAN 1000
004700          AND M-CODE LESS THAN 2001
004800              MOVE M-CODE TO C-CODE
004900              MOVE M-LEVEL TO C-LEVEL
005100              WRITE C-REC.
005200      GO TO C-10.
005300 C-EXIT.
005400      EXIT.
005500 D-END SECTION.
005600 D-10.
005700      CLOSE MASTER-FILE COPY-FILE.
005800 D-EXIT.
005900      EXIT.
```

The difference is quite dramatic. And although the dBASE language was based on the labour-saving features of a database, it extended the labour-saving approach to cover screen handling and other areas such as commonly used functions, for example converting characters to upper-case.

It was necessary, also, to add certain extra commands which the 'one command at a time' user would not require. Since the programmer is not involved in the action of executing the sequence of commands stored on diskette, he had to have the means of making decisions within the program. In effect this meant that he had to be able to ask a question and, depending on the answer, execute one or another sequence of commands. Thus commands such as IF and DO WHILE were included in the language specification. Eventually dBASE II contained some seventy dBASE commands, and you will find them covered amongst the commands described in Chapter 5. Though the list of commands grew, what remained was the simplicity and ease of using dBASE. Much of this was due to the fact that it is a structured language which lends itself to a logical and structured approach to writing programs. Chapter 2 will go into this aspect of the dBASE language in more detail.

Because dBASE II was written to execute the 'one at a time' commands as they were issued, the sequences of commands which were stored on disk as programs were also executed in original form. In other words dBASE II was written to be an interpreter, like BASIC, not as a compiler such as COBOL where the program has to be converted into machine instructions before execution of the program can begin.

Within a short space of time dBASE II became a very popular programming language on microcomputers and has by now sold hundreds of thousands copies. People with no training in computers suddenly found themselves able to write programs, and use their knowledge of their own particular fields of experience, whether it be the legal profession or window manufacturing, to write applications for themselves or for sale to others in the same profession or trade. Others designed and developed software that could be used as add-ons to dBASE II, such as software to draw graphs directly from data contained in a dBASE II database, or create galley proofs by typesetting directly from such data. A whole marketplace of dBASE II applications and associated software came into being, and Ashton Tate made tens of millions dollars out of their creation.

As you may imagine, however, the competition was not long in coming and other products soon arrived claiming to do more than dBASE II. At the same time, microcomputers based on the 16-bit Intel 8086 and 8088 microprocessor chips began to supplant the computers based on the 8-bit Intel 8080 and Zilog Z80 chips. The entry of IBM with its PC containing a 16-bit 8088 chip supported by the DOS operating system decided matters, and software companies hurriedly converted their products to run on the new generation of microcomputer and the DOS operating system. They also found that the extra addressing capability of the 16-bit microprocessors meant that they could write larger and more sophisticated programs.

Ashton Tate first converted dBASE II to run on 16-bit microcomputers like the IBM PC, and then decided to rewrite dBASE II and to do so in Lattice C, an implementation of the C programming language. This is a high level language that loses few of the features available to the Assembler programmer but has the advantages of faster development and easier maintenance. dBASE II had originally been written in assembly language, and Ashton Tate had been struggling with dBASE II for some time because they had run out of room to make changes and every improvement seemed to create fresh software bugs.

When the new dBASE product was ready, however, they decided to keep the original dBASE II for a few years more (mainly to satisfy the continuing demand of those still using 8-bit computers), and issue the new product as dBASE III. There has never been a dBASE I by the way;

the product was called dBASE II from the outset.

dBASE III had more commands, more functions, and even extra database field types. Moreover, Ashton Tate had managed to overcome some of the more serious dBASE II problems such as very slow multi-indexing. There were also minor language changes such as the use of the command CLEAR to clear the screen instead of the original ERASE command. Otherwise, it was the same dBASE language used in the same way and really no different from that of dBASE II. Ashton Tate had even provided a special program called dCONVERT to convert a complete dBASE II application to dBASE III. This conversion program deals with the dBASE II programs themselves, the database file, the indexes, plus all the other related files. The program conversion is 95% successful, leaving only one or two minor adjustments to be carried out by hand.

What was important about dBASE III was the fact that the dBASE specification had been extended: you could have more fields per database, more memory variables, up to ten database files in use at once, and so forth. Also, as mentioned above, the language itself had been extended through the addition of new commands and functions. Nonetheless, dBASE III remained an interpreter and competitors in the database market delighted in pointing to its poor execution speed.

Meanwhile, other software companies were producing their own versions of the dBASE language. A company called Wordtech released a pseudo compiler called dB Compiler. A pseudo compiler converts a dBASE program into a more compact form which can be executed by a runtime program that accompanies the pseudo compiler. The advantages are speed improvement and independence from the Ashton Tate interpreter.

Another company, called Fox Software, released a dBASE II look-alike called FoxBASE. This was an interpreter which was wholly compatible with dBASE II, but since it was written in the C language it was able to cure many of the problems which had beset dBASE II, such as its long list of bugs and very slow multi-indexing. While FoxBASE was an interpreter that could execute any dBASE II program as it stood, it also allowed you to use twice as many memory variables and an extra 12 fields per record. In addition, FoxBASE had a pseudo compiler for those who were keen to use such devices. One of the most important aspects of this dBASE II look-alike was the fact that it had versions that would run with Unix and Xenix, thereby extending the dBASE II programming language to multi-user minicomputers.

Next the first true compiler for dBASE III arrived on the scene. The Clipper compiler translated dBASE III programs into machine code, so that they could execute much faster. The Clipper compiler also released dBASE users from the need to own dBASE II or dBASE III itself, since the compiled programs were free-standing applications. At the same time, the Clipper compiler extended the dBASE specification again. As in the case of the improvements of dBASE III over dBASE II, there were improvements in the number of memory variables you could have, the number of fields per database, and so forth. There were also a number of extra commands and functions. Equally important, however, was the fact that you could link in external programs and routines. With a compiler and linker the dBASE language found itself on a par with other high level languages: the restrictions imposed by using an interpreter had been removed.

Since then, Ashton Tate have replaced dBASE III with dBASE III PLUS, effectively a new version of dBASE III but with extra functions and extra commands. dBASE III PLUS also has a multi-user version which will run on a personal computer network. Fox Software have announced a dBASE III PLUS look-alike which is expected shortly but was not available for inclusion in this book. This also means that the dBASE III specification is likely to be available for Unix and Xenix systems. The developers of Clipper have also promised a multi-user feature to accompany their compiler.

It can be seen quite clearly from all these developments that the dBASE language will continue to grow. In the course of its development, there has been a transition and change of emphasis from dBASE as a microcomputer database package, competing with other microcomputer database packages, to dBASE as *the* major development tool for developers, both corporate and professional, who are creating personal computer applications. And as we are no longer dealing with single user desktop computers, but with networks of personal computers or multi-user minicomputers, the language will continue to spread upwards to take its place beside longer established programming languages.

In Chapter 2, we will look at the way to approach the programming of a new system, and consider some useful programming techniques as well as the pitfalls you might encounter. Chapter 3 describes how you would go about handing over a dBASE application to users, either within your corporate environment or to purchasers of your application. It also looks at the benefits of upgrading existing applications. Chapter 4 explains the compilation and linkage processes in some detail. Chapter 5 covers individual dBASE commands, while Chapter 6 describes the dBASE functions. Chapter 7 discusses the dBASE language in a multi-user environment. Note, however, that this book does not teach you how to start writing dBASE programs. It concerns the use of the dBASE programming language: how to approach a dBASE application, how to employ good programming techniques, how to avoid common pitfalls, and so forth. If you want to learn how to write dBASE programs, you should consult either *Working with dBASE II* or *dBASE III: a Practical Guide*, both published by Collins.

Chapter Two

Programmimg Techniques and Pitfalls

This chapter will not attempt to teach you how to start writing dBASE programs since that topic has already been covered in the two books mentioned on the previous page. Instead we will be concentrating on programming techniques which will help you to create applications that are easy to develop, easy to change afterwards, reasonably secure against mishap, and not too difficult to understand when you look at them again some months later. We will also look at a number of useful programming techniques and common pitfalls.

It is not within the scope of this book to explain how to conduct a systems analysis exercise. We will therefore assume that you have completed the task of analysing the problem, that you have specified the approach to be used by the computer system which will provide a solution to the problem, and that you have defined both the information to be stored and how each group of information will be linked logically to another. What remains is to discuss how to go about designing and writing the programs which make up the system or application.

We start with the premise that any application may be broken up into logical blocks. In a simple application there will be the entry of information, the opportunity to change information previously entered, a means of looking up a specific item of information, and one or two printed information reports. In a more complex application these simple functional blocks will be expanded by sub-division, for example by having several different kinds of data that may be entered. In either case the various functions may be structured into levels. Thus the top level could look like this :

1. Enter information
2. Change existing information
3. Look up an item of information
4. Produce a printed report

The first item could then be sub-divided into:

1. Enter customer details
2. Enter supplier details
3. Enter sales details
4. Enter purchase details

What we are looking at is a means of structuring an application so that anyone using the application will always start by looking at a general set of choices, each of which leads to another set of choices or to a specific action such as 'Enter customer details'. The list of choices is called a *menu* and if you were to display such a menu on a computer screen, the person using the application could signal his choice by entering the corresponding menu number, for example by entering a '1' to 'Enter information'. The application could then present another menu – that on the next level down – which would invite the user to select the type of information to be entered. While we are looking at menus, you may like to remember that it is important to provide every menu with an Exit option so that the user may return either to the previous menu or to the operating system.

The nice thing about the menu approach is that when it comes to programming, you can break up your programs into the same structure. You would typically start by having a program that does no more than present the top level menu. Each option on the top level menu would result in another program, either one that carries out a specific action such as allowing the user to make changes to previously entered information, or one that presents another menu of choices. In the latter case, each option would again result in a program which performs the function indicated by that option. We are thus, by looking at the application through the user's eyes, structuring it and defining the various program modules that will be required, for example:

Main menu (program 1):
1. Enter information (program 2)
2. Change existing information (program 3)
3. Look up an item of information (program 4)
4. Produce a printed report (program 5)

First sub-menu: Enter Information

1. Enter customer details (program 6)
2. Enter supplier details (program 7)
3. Enter sales details (program 8)
4. Enter purchase details (program 9)

Each program will be contained in a command or program file and since, as is apparent from the small example above, we will soon have a multitude of program files, we need to give some thought to the naming of these files. Ideally we want a method of naming whereby a program filename will immediately tell you where it belongs in the application structure. Let us decide on a convention whereby the application is identified by either two characters or four characters, for example FA for fixed assets, or, to use a more colloquial approach, CARS for a fleet management application.

Next we call our top level menu program by this name, thus FA.PRG or CARS.PRG. The programs which lead from this menu could thus be called FAA.PRG, FAB.PRG, FAC.PRG, FAD.PRG or CARS1.PRG, CARS2.PRG, CARS3.PRG, CARS4.PRG. Let us follow the CARS approach, so that the program names are as follows:

Main menu (CARS.PRG):
   1. Enter information (CARS1.PRG)
   2. Change existing information (CARS2.PRG)
   3. Look up an item of information (CARS3.PRG)
   4. Produce a printed report (CARS4.PRG)

Where CARS1.PRG produces a sub-menu, we simply extend the naming scheme by adding a further digit:

First sub-menu: Enter Information (CARS1.PRG)
   1. Enter customer details (CARS11.PRG)
   2. Enter supplier details (CARS12.PRG)
   3. Enter sales details (CARS13.PRG)
   4. Enter purchase details (CARS14.PRG)

This particular naming convention can go to four levels of sub-menu. If your system is very sophisticated so that you need more, choose a two character identification such as CA instead. You may also find that you cannot use digits because your menus run to more than nine options, in which case you would list your menu alphabetically and use the letters of the alphabet in your naming convention:

Main menu (CARS.PRG):
   A.   Enter information (CARSA.PRG)
   B.   Change existing information (CARSB.PRG)
   C.   Look up an item of information (CARSC.PRG)
   D.   Produce a printed report (CARSD.PRG)

Let us next look at a method of programming such a menu-based approach. The examples in this chapter are all based on the dBASE III specification, but you should be able to follow them with no difficulty even if you are using the dBASE II specification:

```
do while .t.
  clear
  store ' ' to option
  a 1,0 say 'FLEET MANAGEMENT'
  a 5,0 say '1. Enter information'
  a 6,0 say '2. Change existing information'
  a 7,0 say '3. Look up an item of information'
  a 8,0 say '4. Produce a printed report'
  a 9,0 say 'X. Exit'
  a 13,0 say 'Enter your choice ' get option picture '!'
  read
  do case
    case option = 'X'
      clear
      quit
    case option = '1'
      do cars1
    case option = '2'
      do cars2
    case option = '3'
      do cars3
    case option = '4'
      do cars4
  endcase
enddo
```

In a real life program you would no doubt improve on the actual menu text used, but in our example we will leave it as it is so that it conforms to the text already in use. Before we look at the routine itself, notice the use of indentation to show the logical structure of the program.

The example falls into three sections contained within a permanent DO loop. The first section displays the menu on the screen, the second section consists of just the READ command which accepts the user's reply, and the third calls the appropriate sub-program according to the user's reply. If the user had selected an invalid option, i.e. by replying with anything other than the digits 1 to 4 or the character X, control would return to the beginning of the DO loop and the complete sequence of displaying menu text, reading the reply, and so on would be repeated. In a simple display such as that shown above this may not matter, but if you were to improve the presentation of your menu, for example by surrounding the text with a box, the user would find the continual redisplay of the menu slow and irritating. A slightly different technique could then be employed, such as one which reduces the redisplay to just one line:

```
do while .t.
  clear
  store ' ' to option
  @ 1,0 say 'FLEET MANAGEMENT'
  @ 5,0 say '1. Enter information'
  @ 6,0 say '2. Change existing information'
  @ 7,0 say '3. Look up an item of information'
  @ 8,0 say '4. Produce a printed report'
  @ 9,0 say 'X. Exit'
  do while .not. option$'1234X'
    @ 13,0 say 'Enter your choice ' get option picture '!'
    read
  enddo
  do case
    case option = 'X'
      clear
      quit
    case option = '1'
      do cars1
    case option = '2'
      do cars2
    case option = '3'
      do cars3
    case option = '4'
      do cars4
  endcase
enddo
```

This technique relies on using a DO loop that will repeat the commands within the loop until a valid reply has been received. The substring comparison operator $ will return a logical True and thus exit the DO loop only if the user's reply matches one of the characters in the string '1234X'. In the example this technique accomplishes the objective of not displaying the menu and associated text unnecessarily, but it is equally important as a method of preventing program crashes. One of the most common causes of crashes lies in receiving unexpected replies from a user, and this technique allows you to specify precisely what may or may not be entered.

The technique is especially useful when you are expecting a Yes/No reply. Programmers will often fall into the trap of simply testing for a Yes, and assume that if the response was not Yes, a No must have been entered. By ensuring that the program can only receive a Yes or a No you avoid following such false trails:

```
if reply$"YyNn"
```

While on the subject of the substring comparison operator, you should be careful of its use when you are allowing the user to reply with more than one character. If, for example, you are expecting any one of only four sales regions which are NW,SW,NE and SE you might write your routine as follows and confidently expect no further problems:

```
do while .not. region$"NWSWNESE"
  @ 13,0 say 'Enter your choice ' get region picture '!!'
  read
enddo
```

Supposing, though, that the user entered ES? The string ES is clearly contained within the comparison string and would thus pass the test employed by the DO loop. It shows that you can never be too careful. There are ways of improving the test so that accidental user replies are still trapped, for example by using the substring search function to test that the substring starts on an uneven letter in the comparison string:

```
do while AT(region,"NWSWNESE")/2 = int(AT(region,"NWSWNESE")/2)
```

But in the end these tests get so complicated that they become silly and you find yourself better off employing a more long-winded test such as comparing for every region specifically. The important point being made here is not that of finding a clever error trapping technique, but of making certain that you think about all such potentially risky situations and that you provide adequate precautions against them. In the course of the rest of this chapter we will look at other potential pitfalls, but let us for the moment return to the structure of the program.

In a structured programming language like dBASE, there are no labels that can be used to point to certain parts of your program, nor are there Branch or Goto instructions for transferring control to such labelled parts. This means that you are placing large blocks of your program logic within the boundaries represented by conditional commands such as IF and ENDIF pairs, or IF, ELSE, and ENDIF sets. In a complex program you may start feeling that you are losing control because of the number of levels to which you are nesting conditions within other conditions. The problem usually takes the form of losing visual control: if the tests could all be seen at a glance, even if tests were nested within tests to four or five levels deep, you would be able to assimilate the logic at once. For this reason, the DO command is a favourite method of reducing to simpler terms the logic of a program. It is used to remove large blocks of your program to .PRG disk files, from where they may be called up during execution without getting in the way of your comprehension of the program.

In the dBASE III specification you can improve on this by using a procedure file which contains all the sub-program blocks that you expect to use in any one section of the program. Each block is headed by the PROCEDURE command and the name of the sub-program. The procedure file itself is simply another .PRG file which is read from disk when you issue the SET PROCEDURE TO command. After this all the procedures or sub-program blocks it contains will be more readily available than if they resided on disk as separate .PRG files.

Continuing the topic of program structure, you should also ensure that each sub-program contains a RETURN command which transfers control back to the sub-program at the next level up or to the starting menu program. The latter will probably finish its activities with the QUIT command so that the user is returned to the DOS environment.

The positioning of RETURN commands may be discussed briefly. Where there is a menu display within the sub-program, the RETURN command will be situated to take effect immediately it is identified that the user wants to take the Exit option of the menu, possibly pausing just long enough to issue a clear screen command first. Otherwise the RETURN command will typically be positioned at the end of the sub-program, for example following the last ENDDO. You should also remember when you issue the RETURN command that in the dBASE III specification, the memory variables you have created within the sub-program will automatically be released unless you specifically defined them as PUBLIC. This is an important caution for programmers who have grown accustomed in dBASE II to setting indicators in one sub-program and testing them elsewhere, either at a higher level or in other sub-programs on different branches of the menu tree. Memory variables will, of course, remain intact when you move from one sub-program to another at a lower level, for example from CARS1.PRG to CARS11.PRG or CARS12.PRG.

You will have noticed that much of what has been said above has been directed at creating programs that are easy to read and understand. The less confusing a program, the faster it can be developed and the easier it is to maintain afterwards. Another important contribution to program clarity lies in the careful use of explanatory text within a program. In addition to being able to use NOTE or * commands, you may add comments to certain program lines. These include lines containing ENDIF, ENDDO, ENDCASE and SELECT commands. The text you add to such lines could be explanations to remind you of the function of the DO loop or IF test, or you could repeat the condition that controls the DO loop or IF test, for example:

```
do while .not. option$'1234X'
   a 13,0 say 'Enter your choice ' get option picture '!'
   read
enddo [.not. option$'1234X']
```

In an example where the beginning of the structure can be seen in the same glance as the end of the structure this probably seems superfluous, but in many applications the two are often separated by a large number of lines. Also, you will often find that several ENDDO and ENDIF lines occur close together so that you need to rely heavily on indentation to make sense of the program structure. In such cases, the addition of a comment that reminds you of the test controlling the pair will be invaluable. In the dBASE III PLUS specification you may use the & & command to add comments to lines other than those mentioned above.

Let us next look at a few of the pitfalls that lie in wait for unsuspecting users and the means of preventing them. One of the most common situations to be found in a dBASE program is that the most recently used .DBF file is left open after use. The reason is that when you start a sub-program you would issue the USE command to open the file, but upon completing the sub-program, you would simply return to the menu. If the user did not exit from the main menu, the .DBF file plus any associated index and other files would remain open until another USE command in another sub-program is issued. By its nature a menu would be displayed for long periods of time, awaiting the next choice which might be some time later. During such a period there will be no opportunity to close the file, which leaves you a potential victim to one of the most illogical features of both the dBASE II and dBASE III interpreters: until a file is closed, the 'Number of files in the database' field in the database header is not updated. This means that a sudden power surge or an accidental power failure or hardware breakdown during the menu inactive period could lose you valuable data. Imagine having just spent an hour bringing your files bang up to date, only to find an hour later that the hour's work has all been lost because of a freak accident. The safe thing to do is to close your files immediately after use. Taking the latter first, you could issue a general USE command in dBASE II or the CLOSE DATA command in dBASE III at the start of each menu. You may even prefer to reset all conditions including files by issuing the dBASE II CLEAR command or dBASE III CLEAR ALL command.

Another area that requires attention is that of limitations within the interpreter. An obvious one is that of the maximum number of memory variables as well as the maximum amount of memory that may be allocated to memory variables. In dBASE II, for example, you can easily exhaust the amount of space reserved for memory variables without getting anywhere near the limit of 64 variables. Try having 20 variables of 80 characters each. The sad thing about the dBASE II interpreter is that when it meets a condition it cannot handle, such as 20 80-character variables, it simply gives up and returns you to the dot prompt. In dBASE III, the maximum number of variables has been increased to 256, and in the Clipper compiler you may have 2048 variables. dBASE III allows 6000 bytes for its memory variables, but the amount of memory may be increased by setting the MVARSIZ option in the CONFIG.DB file.

Another trap lies in the indiscriminate or repeated use of the @ GET command. dBASE II will allow only 64 GETS while dBASE III allows 128. In the latter instance, and given sufficient memory, you may increase the number of GETS to 1023 through the use of the CONFIG.DB file. A much simpler tactic, however, is to release the GETS that are no longer required. This involves you in no more than issuing the CLEAR GETS command after you have finished with a particular menu, for example after you have ascertained to your satisfaction that you have received a valid reply in response to the menu options. In the example given earlier, the command would be positioned as follows:

```
do while .not. option$'1234X'
  a 13,0 say 'Enter your choice ' get option picture '!'
  read
enddo
clear gets
do case
```

There is also the trap of relying on the existence of a file and then finding that someone has deleted the file. You may, for example, consider the line below to be reasonably foolproof:

```
use cars index make
```

However, the .DBF or the .NDX file may go missing because a user had unintentionally deleted it with a DOS command. When the interpreter fails to find a file it will complain, and if the user cannot remedy the situation, the dot prompt will appear. The way to control such a situation is to test for the existence of files so that you can issue an intelligent message to the user or even recreate the file yourself:

```
store "make.ndx" to fname
if .not. file(fname)
  ? "Index file MAKE missing : now recreating it"
  set talk on
  index on make+model to make
  set talk off
else
  set index to make
endif
```

The reason for the SET TALK ON command is to allow the user to view the progress of the indexing operation rather than just making him wait without knowing what is happening. Another file that can go missing is the .DBT Memo file. You may, for example, use the COPY FILE command to create a copy of your database and forget to copy the .DBT file as well. The COPY TO command is safer since it will copy both the database and the associated Memo file.

The INDEX command and its associates FIND and SEEK are also full of opportunities for getting it wrong. For example, if you are indexing a character field it will be safer to use the upper-case function when you create the index so that all index entries will be in the same case:

```
index on upper(make+model) to make
```

At the same time, you would use the upper-case PICTURE clause in your @ GET commands to ensure that the names given to you by the user are also in upper-case. Another fairly common error occurs when you index a combination of numeric and character fields, such as:

```
index on str(chequeno,4)+name to payees
```

If we assume that we want to look up a record containing the cheque number 0005, we would probably use the STR function once again:

```
. store str(5,4) to keyval
. find &keyval
no find

. store "1234" to xx
. display memory
KEYVAL      (C)      5
XX          (C)   1234
** TOTAL **      02 VARIABLES USED   00008 BYTES USED
```

The second part of the example has been provided simply to demonstrate that the digit 5 is correctly positioned within the variable KEYVAL, i.e. exactly where it would be in the index entry. So why did the FIND command fail? The reason lies in the use of the & macro: before being executed the command line passes through a preliminary process whereby any words which are prefixed by & are replaced by the contents of the fields referenced by those words. The FIND line will thus translate to:

```
. find    5
```

Note the size of the gap between the FIND command itself and the digit 5: it quite properly includes the three blank characters created by the STR function. Unfortunately dBASE, in looking for the character string that the FIND command is to operate on, does not mind how many spaces there are between the word FIND and the character string. As a result the FIND command will look for an index entry that starts with the character '5' not the character string '   5'. The answer to this problem is to use the SEEK command which does not require the & macro usage, since it expects a variable name rather than the string itself. In dBASE II, which does not have the SEEK command, you should place the expression within quotes:

```
. store str(5,4) to keyval
. find "&keyval"
```

The use of macros can sometimes make a program look confusing, but provided you remember that macro substitution briefly alters the program line itself and nothing else, you should have no difficulties with it. All you have to do is try to imagine how the program line would look after the substitution has taken place. Any other difficulties you have with macro substitution will be related to different implementations of the use of macros by the interpreters and compilers, and these are usually well publicised in fault reports or differences summaries. To give an example, the dBASE III implementation of macro substitution on the DO WHILE command line can cause problems because dBASE III attempts to improve execution speed of the DO loop. It does so by analysing the DO WHILE expression only on the first occasion that it executes the DO loop, saving the pointers to the variables used in the expression for any subsequent times that execution passes back to the beginning of the DO loop. This means that changes made to a memory variable within the DO loop will not be applied to a corresponding macro variable on the DO WHILE command line.

In the remaining pages of this chapter a number of suggestions and cautions are raised, but only briefly since each refers you to a dBASE command or function which may be explored in more detail by reading the appropriate section in Chapter 5 or 6. For example, if you are using the ACCEPT command you should be particularly careful to test for a correct response. In the dBASE III specification, if the user simply presses the Return key in response to an ACCEPT command, a null variable will be generated. Also, like the STORE command, the ACCEPT command can change the type of an existing memory variable which can lead to problems later in the program. Since the ACCEPT command carries potential risks, and the INPUT command is too unpredictable to be used safely, it may be wise to restrict yourself to the use of @ GET commands instead.

Leaving the dangers aside for a moment, there are many ways of improving the presentation of a dBASE application. Let us start by looking at some of the commands that affect screen output. One of the simplest is to enclose your menu or input areas by drawing a box on the screen. A group of @ SAY commands may be used, but in dBASE III

PLUS and in the Clipper compiler you have respectively the @ TO and the @ BOX commands, either of which are capable of producing a box from a single command. And on the subject of displaying menus, you can improve on the usual @ SAY and @ GET approach by using the @ PROMPT and MENU TO commands of the Clipper compiler. These allow the user a Lotus style method whereby options can be highlighted in turn by means of the arrow keys, until one is accepted by pressing the Return key. The @ PROMPT command also provides you with the means of displaying separately a different message as each option is highlighted. Another way of improving screen presentation is to use the SET COLOR TO command. On a monochrome screen this command may be used to create underlining or a reverse video effect.

If we look at general presentation, either on screen or printer, the following may improve matters. The PICTURE clause in the @ SAY GET command has a large range of formatting characters that may be used to show the information in a natural way, for example by breaking up large values with commas or stops, or enclosing negative values in parentheses. The drawback of the @ SAY command is that its output cannot be written to a disk file, for example as a means of passing on information reports not on paper but on diskette.

In the dBASE III PLUS specification, the TRANSFORM function will extend the formatting features of @ SAY to commands like ?, LIST, and REPORT. Another command that should be used whenever possible is the SET DATE command which will produce a date familiar to a particular nationality, for example SET DATE BRITISH to obtain DD/MM/YY in all date displays. Another date convention that you may care to observe is to use the DAY( ), CMONTH( ), and YEAR( ) functions to obtain the date in expanded format, for example:

```
store date()             to today
store str(day(today),2)  to dd
store cmonth(today)      to mm
store str(year(today),4) to yy
? dd,mm,yy
```

19 August 1986

When creating printed output, you should consider the use of enlarged characters for headings, or condensed characters for long print lines, for example to squeeze 132 characters onto 80 column paper. The printer control code will vary from printer to printer, but if we take the Epson standard which is also that used by the IBM printer, we find that the ASCII representation of the numeric value 15 signals condensed print. The SET PRINT ON command followed by ? CHR(15) will send the necessary control code to the printer. Another way of sending control codes to a printer is to use the Escape code of CHR(27) followed by the appropriate codes. For example, condensed print on an Epson can also be obtained by the following:

```
set talk off
set print on
store chr(27)+"!"+chr(4) to modex
? modex
set print off
set talk on
return
```

Let us look at some other control codes that can be sent by means of the CHR(27) Escape code. If we want large banner sized characters, we can send the code CHR(56):

```
store chr(27)+"!"+chr(56) to modex
? modex
```

Similarly, Elite print can be obtained as follows:

```
store chr(27)+"M" to modex
? modex
```

Even when we look at a sophisticated laser printer such as the HP LaserJet, we find we can still configure the printer by means of the Escape code followed by control characters:

```
set talk off
store chr(27)+chr(40)+chr(115) to modex1
store chr(49)+chr(54)+chr(46)  to modex2
store chr(54)+chr(72)          to modex3
store modex1+modex2+modex3     to modex
set print on
? modex
* This sets up a pitch of 16.66 cpi on the LaserJet+
set print off
return
```

The printer control codes will usually be found in your printer manual. What the above illustrates is that you can use dBASE commands and functions to obtain any of the special printer settings available through software control.

If we broaden the scope of useful suggestions, we should consider the use of the ON ERROR command in the dBASE III PLUS specification, coupled with the MESSAGE( ) function to trap errors and provide both an explanation and graceful exit from error conditions. Another useful function is the MEMOEDIT( ) function of the Clipper compiler which allows a user to examine and change Memo fields under program control. Still on the subject of Clipper, you might wish to use its DTOS( ) function to index a date field in the form YYYYMMDD.

Another very useful function is INKEY( ) which allows you to test for user interruptions. You could, for example during a long print operation, use this function as a constant check to find out whether the user wants to abort the operation. Then there are the dBASE III PLUS RECSIZE( ) and RECCOUNT( ) functions which, when multiplied, provide you with the approximate size of your database. See the description of the RECSIZE( ) function for a completely accurate method of calculating the size of a database of the dBASE III specification. The database size may be compared with the number of bytes returned by the DISKSPACE( ) function to find out if there is sufficient room to create a security copy of a database file.

You may also like to be aware of a method for creating a database file from within your program, by using the COPY STRUCTURE EXTENDED command followed by CREATE FROM. And in dBASE III PLUS you can write and read directly to and from spreadsheet files such as a 1-2-3 .WKS file by using respectively the COPY TO and APPEND FROM commands.

The points mentioned above represent some of the items covered in the individual descriptions of the commands and functions given in Chapters 5 and 6. These descriptions are intended not as a dBASE reference but as a means of drawing attention to the way in which each of these commands or functions can be used within a dBASE program, together with notes on implementation differences in the various dBASE language products described in the Chapter 1.

Chapter Three

Giving a dBASE System to Users

When we have completed the job of developing a dBASE application, ready to hand it over to our users or sell it on the open market, we still have several issues to consider. We have to decide what form the programs will take, how to package the application, and what user support we will provide. Let us look at each of these issues in turn, starting with the dBASE programs themselves.

These we can hand over in any of the following forms:

- dBASE source form
- RunTime form
- Tokenised form
- Compiled form

In dBASE source form, the programs are issued to users as text files in .PRG form, exactly as they were while we were developing them. The programs will be executed by one of the interpreters, i.e. dBASE II, FoxBASE, dBASE III, or dBASE III PLUS. We would thus need to ensure that each potential user has a copy of the appropriate interpreter. We would explain to the users the need to load the interpreter prior to starting the application, or we would set up a DOS batch file containing the necessary commands to do so.

Of course this means that each user incurs the cost of an extra copy of the interpreter. In the case of dBASE III PLUS this runs to nearly £600 at the time of writing. It also means that each user has to sacrifice the disk space occupied by the interpreter and, more worrying, that users are able to meddle with the application. Since the application is held in text form as dBASE source, it is quite easy for anyone who has a smattering of the dBASE language to make minor changes to the application by using a word processor or even the dBASE editor itself. We will be discussing the support of applications in a moment, but consider how difficult it must be to find the cause of a problem that has suddenly arisen because someone has quietly and inexpertly meddled with your dBASE programs.

And yet, even with these disadvantages of extra cost and loss of disk space and exposure to tampering, a great many dBASE applications are issued in exactly this way. Recognising the problems, Ashton Tate produced a remedy called RunTime.

RunTime was initially available only for dBASE II and consisted of two programs, dBCode and dBRun. dBCode compressed and encrypted dBASE programs so that they could not be listed in intelligible form or indeed modified. The second program, dBRun, executed the compressed application without requiring dBASE II itself to be present. However, RunTime operates on a license basis whereby a fixed number of encrypted copies are bought. The cost per copy is negotiable and naturally depends on volume, but a license for five copies might cost you £50 per copy.

dBASE III initially had no runtime feature, so that each user of an application written in dBASE III was forced to buy a copy of dBASE III itself. Eventually, a special version of dBASE III called the Developers' Release containing a runtime arrangement was announced, although at a considerably higher price per copy than that of dBASE II. Applications for a runtime license are made direct to Ashton Tate.

Another form of issuing dBASE applications consists of using a pseudo compiler. This approach first tokenises the dBASE programs and then uses a runtime program to unscramble and execute the tokenised code. Tokenising simply means that the dBASE source is scanned and all keywords are replaced by single character tokens. Variable names, i.e. names other than dBASE keywords, are placed into a name table, and the relative position of the variable in the name table is used to replace the variable name itself in the source line.

The resulting code is thus very compact and quite unreadable to the casual eye. It does, however, require a special runtime program to decode it and, of course, to execute it. An example of such a tokenising approach is that available as an extra with FoxBASE, a dBASE II look-alike interpreter. Another dBASE II tokeniser is dB Compiler by Wordtech. Each user still needs to purchase the runtime program so the cost element remains a problem.

Finally, there is the true dBASE compiler. A true compiler as opposed to a peudo compiler will translate dBASE source programs into machine code, i.e. into instructions that can be executed directly by the computer's microprocessor. Obviously a single dBASE command such as INDEX will result in a large number of microprocessor instructions, but being specific to the dBASE language the compiler is geared to produce all of these when it encounters the dBASE command.

A compiler program will read in the dBASE programs making up an application, translate them, and then write out a file containing the equivalent microprocessor instructions. If the dBASE application covers more than one dBASE program file, the compiler will pull them all together as it performs the translation of the application into machine code.

By tradition, a compiler requires an extra step called a linker. This consists of another program which reads in the file created by the compiler and resolves any loose ends. For example, one dBASE program might CALL another entirely separate program or routine (see Chapter 4). It is the linker's job to combine the two into a single executable program in .COM or .EXE form.

At the time of writing the only true compiler on the market was a dBASE III compiler called Clipper. There were several linkers available, including the PC-DOS LINK program, but the Clipper compiler has its own linker which is a specially adapted version of a popular linker called Plink86.

Since, after using a true compiler and a linker, the application is in the form of a stand alone executable .EXE program, the application needs neither the dBASE interpreter nor the runtime equivalent. There is thus no extra cost to users in the sense of having to pay for an interpreter or runtime support system. And since users receive only the machine code, they are unable to meddle with the programs or even to examine the source code making up the application.

There are merits in all four approaches to handing over your application, whether in dBASE source form, with Ashton Tate's RunTime system, in tokenised form, or as a .EXE program; it depends on your situation and your users. You may prefer to keep the application in dBASE source form to enable you to apply quick remedies on the spot when unforeseen problems are encountered. Or you may have a large number of users where cost becomes paramount and where a no-cost .EXE version of the application is the obvious choice.

Packaging an application

Packaging is a term that refers to the dressing up of an application that you intend to sell. It covers the physical appearance of the box or container, the production of a user manual, the style of the documentation, the logo of your company and of the product name, the method whereby the diskette(s) containing the application is held within the container, and so forth.

These issues will not be material to all dBASE users. However, whether we are discussing an application that is to be sold or one that will simply be distributed within a corporate environment, the one element that is vital to both is to prepare some form of documentation for the intended users of the application. Documentation for customers usually tends to be more comprehensive since there is less opportunity for personal explanations on an 'as the need arises' basis. To avoid discussing two standards of documentation it will be easier if we concentrate on the higher of the two requirements, and leave you to water it down as seems appropriate for your own environment.

A user manual should start with an introduction to the application to give the user a starting reference point. Next it should explain to the uninitiated how to load the application, and how to exit from it. There are a surprising number of software products which leave the new user high and dry when it comes to knowing how to return to DOS other than by switching off the computer. Of course, if you are using a menu approach with Exit as one of the menu options, there should be no problem.

Next the manual should take each part of the application and explain it both in terms of purpose and use. Certain aspects which might be self-evident to the developer may floor the user completely, for example when you have been adding records how do you return to the main menu? Cursor controls should be explained, and there should be some guidance on how to correct mistakes. New users have little confidence and are usually very afraid that they might be damaging the computer system, thereby inviting unwelcome criticism of their efforts.

The manual should also list and explain error messages and the appropriate corrective actions. Wherever possible the language used in this kind of documentation should be basic English, with a colloquial touch for friendliness, much as one would use in talking to a very bright child. Computerese or stilted English merely serves to alienate and confuse the reader.

Another aspect of the manual is presentation, which refers to the design of the text layout including the font chosen to set the text. Users are put off by page after page of tightly packed text. An open layout with large margins, frequent headings, examples, and even illustrations is far more likely to persuade the user to consult the manual. Another attractive feature, particularly for users unfamiliar with the application, is an index to the manual.

As regards the rest of the packaging process, you would be well advised to approach a printer for help on designing the physical appearance of your package: the type of binder, the colours used, the logo or style of your product name and even of your company name, the typeface to be used for printing the manual, and so forth.

Binders come in many shapes, and expense will dictate the type you choose. The cheapest is probably a rigid plastic spine that simply clamps the pages together. The drawback with this method is that the manual cannot be laid open for easy reference while you work, and the pages have a tendency to slip out. Then there is wire or saddle stitching (stapling) which is frequently used in magazines but which limits the number of pages you can safely combine. Next is plastic or wire comb binding, similar to spiral binding. It is practical and allows the booklet to lie open easily. You may not think it stylish enough, in which case you might want to consider 'perfect binding' which involves a glued spine, often against cloth, much as you would find in a paperback book. This is quite attractive but, as with paperbacks, such a manual again may not lie open very easily. With all of these the diskettes containing the application could either be placed in pockets which form part of the inside front or back cover or, as is sometimes the case, simply be placed loose inside the booklet. The whole may then be shrink-wrapped to ensure that it is received in mint condition by the end user.

A ring binder with two or three rings and covered in either cloth or plastic is a favourite way of packaging computer software, but is usually accompanied by a slip case or library box which tends to be expensive. The binder or slip case manufacturer will want to know what page size you have selected for your manual and how many pages you expect to include in a copy, and will then advise you on the binder specification such as width of the spine and so forth. The manufacturer will also take care of printing your product and company logo on the binder and slip case. Provision for diskettes is made either by supplying a separate plastic page which contains one or more pockets or by including a plastic or cardboard pocket as part of the inside front or back cover.

The next step will be to have your text typeset and printed. Any printer will take care of this job, but you should insist on specifying the layout of the text very carefully for the reasons explained earlier in this chapter. An inexpensive method of producing copies of a manual consists of printing the original with a letter quality printer and making copies on a high quality photocopier. You will not, however, be able to disguise the fact that you have economised at the expense of quality. For a small number of copies you might also consider the use of a laser printer with the advantage of being able to achieve considerable variation in the typeface.

Since the cost of producing your manuals may be quite high, it is important that you first research your market carefully to assure yourself that you will recover your investment. Unless you have approached it as a business venture by employing staff to develop your application, your development effort may be seen in the same context as any other spare time occupation that is carried out for enjoyment rather than profit. It is only when you start packaging your application that you find yourself spending money that would not otherwise have been spent.

User support

If we assume that we have satisfactorily dealt with the problem of how to issue the application to users, we next have to consider how to support these same users. You may think that you have tested the application to the point where nothing can go wrong, but if you do you are fooling yourself.

Users are quite brilliant at finding ways of upsetting the application simply because they have not been trained to respond in a conditioned way. Instead they do whatever seems reasonable at the time, for example they press the Escape key which, with the dBASE II or dBASE III interpreter, instantly returns an application to the dot prompt and confuses the users totally. Chapter 2 discussed several of these common pitfalls, but you may depend on it that some user somewhere will find one that you have not covered. It makes sense, therefore, to set up a user support service, even if it exists only to analyse and correct user problems such as being confronted by a blank screen because the screen plug has worked itself loose at the back of a PC system unit.

Such a support service is also self protective, since there is a better than average chance that you will find a user struggling to employ a valid condition which your system refuses to accept: something that you somehow managed to overlook when you developed the application.

So how does one provide user support? At the simplest level it means that someone has to be available to receive calls from users, either in person or by telephone. Ideally such a person will know enough about dBASE and the application to discuss the problem intelligently. Alternatively, the support person would take a message and give the promise that someone will call back to investigate the problem. In either case, the support person would keep a record of the date, time, user name and telephone number, and a description of the problem. Later, when the problem has been resolved, the completion date and time and a brief description of the remedy would be added.

Such a fault log serves two purposes. In the first place it ensures that user problems are not ignored or overlooked. Secondly, it acts as a means of identifying frequently occurring problems. It will save you and your users much time if you take the trouble to document such problems and the recommended course of action, and regularly circulate all users with these reports.

If you feel surprised that so much support might be necessary, just reflect on the fact that we are discussing a situation where users are left on their own with very sophisticated desk top computers (and no computer staff to protect the machine), with mechanical devices called printers which rarely behave themselves, and with your application which may or may not be user-proof. The scope for unforeseen difficulties is enormous. Another way of providing user support is to provide training. In the more complex applications training before use will be essential. In others it may be possible to rely on the user manual that accompanies the application. Generally, however, users will be more successful in their use of an application if someone has gently guided them through on a personal basis, with opportunity for answering individual questions or giving explanations where there is obvious uncertainty.

Upgrading

This section is concerned with the question of trying to improve your application not by extensive rewriting but by changing the software that executes the application. If you are a dBASE II developer you may consider whether to convert your applications from dBASE II to dBASE III which is more powerful, or to a different dBASE II interpreter such as FoxBASE which does not have a multi-indexing problem or which, if you wish, will allow you to run your application under Unix. If you are a dBASE III user you may be considering the potential benefits of using a compiler.

The dBASE III interpreter is an obvious upgrade for dBASE II developers, so let us begin by looking at good reasons why you should *not* upgrade a dBASE II application to dBASE III. First of all, if you or your users are using a personal computer which does not have a hard disk so that the amount of space consumed by the software on the floppy drives becomes crucial, dBASE II (which requires only about a quarter of the diskette space available on one IBM PC drive) is far more practical than dBASE III. Secondly, without breaking the license agreements, you can have a separate copy of dBASE II on each applications diskette so that a diskette that contains the software can also be used for index or other similar applications files. With dBASE III, the software is copy protected so that it has to be installed on a particular diskette. This naturally limits the use of that diskette. Of course, on hard disk systems both of these concerns carry considerably less weight and there is little reason for not using dBASE III in place of dBASE II. A third reason for not converting to dBASE III is that it requires at least 256 Kbytes of memory against the 128 Kbytes of dBASE II (on the IBM PC and compatibles). Finally, you may have invested in a number of copies of dBASE II for your users and would not want to incur the expenditure of replacing these with dBASE III copies.

If we look at the reasons why you *should* upgrade a dBASE II application, we find that there are several. One of the most obvious reasons relates to the indexing problem of dBASE II. Although the dBASE II specification covers the use of up to six index files at the same time, few applications attempt to use more than one during file maintenance because of the dramatic way in which it slows down the application. There have been many attempts by the dBASE II software team at Ashton Tate to cure the problem, but what they were up against was the fact that dBASE II is written in the Assembler language and, with the software at the limit of the memory segment size, they ran out of room to make changes. This was also the reason for their inability to cure the continuing series of software bugs with which dBASE II has been plagued. Another restriction in dBASE II is the fact that you can have only 64 memory variables, a limitation that has caused programmers many headaches. Finally, Ashton Tate have announced that the life of the dBASE II interpreter as a product will be coming to an end before much longer. There is thus no prospect of future improvement, and finding support may become a problem.

Before looking at dBASE III as an obvious upgrade route, we might consider those of you who are not in the least inclined to change from the dBASE II specification but would like a solution to one or two of the most telling dBASE II problems. Here, the upgrade path could lead to the use of the FoxBASE interpreter which, like dBASE III, is written in the C language, a high level language that makes changes an easier matter so that bugs become less of a problem. Also, this implementation of the dBASE II specification has overcome the multi-indexing problem. FoxBASE will execute any dBASE II program without change, but if you want to improve on the dBASE II specification FoxBASE will allow you twice as many memory variables and an extra 12 fields per database. In addition, there is a FoxBASE pseudo compiler which you may use if you want faster execution. FoxBASE will also let you run your dBASE II application in a multi-user environment under Unix or Xenix.

Let us next turn to the attractions of dBASE III. One good reason why you should convert to dBASE III is the fact that the latter has a specification which exceeds that of dBASE II by a large margin. For example, dBASE III will let you have 128 fields compared with the 32 of dBASE II, 256 memory variables compared with 64, a billion records compared with 65 000 and so forth. dBASE III also introduced two new field types: the Date and the Memo fields, the latter a useful means of recording free textual information in association with a particular record in the database. Another important aspect of the dBASE III specification is that it allows you to have more than 2 database files open at the same time, in fact up to 10 at once. In addition there is the automatic means (SET RELATION) of relating information from one database to another, for example relating a database containing names and addresses to one containing sales information, so that when you find the particular record on the names database, the sales database will automatically be moved on to reflect the corresponding sales details.

The actual task of converting from dBASE II to dBASE III is reasonably simple. Included in the dBASE III software is a utility program called dCONVERT which will convert all the files concerned with a dBASE II application. It is somewhat rudimentary in the sense that you have to specify each file yourself, even to the extent of converting each program file individually, but in the end you will have had an automatic conversion of 95% of your application. Index files are not converted as such; instead dCONVERT produces a program file that contains the appropriate INDEX instruction for each index file. The idea is that after you have converted the database file, you will run these program files through dBASE III to set up the indexes. The remainder of the unsuccessful conversion resides mainly in having to look through your converted program files to see if there are any tricky bits of code that could not be converted. One such example concerns the use of the STR function to create a large memory variable containing spaces:

```
store str(1,41) to spaces
store $(spaces,40) to namex
```

dCONVERT, unable to fathom such illicit use of a function, will simply convert the substring function name from $ to SUBSTR and leave the rest alone. Unfortunately, dBASE III behaves differently and you will not get 40 spaces out of the resulting code. What you have to do is delete the first line and change the second to make use of a legitimate dBASE III alternative, the SPACE function:

```
store space(40) to spacex
```

Apart from such special situations, the rest of the conversion is quite automatic and you should be able to convert and test an entire dBASE II application in a matter of hours.

The next question concerns whether you should upgrade a dBASE III application. The most obvious way of upgrading from dBASE III is to compile the application. There are four major reasons for wanting to do so: speed improvement, cost savings, improved language specification, and the flexibility gained from being able to link in external routines.

The speed at which an application operates may or may not be a consideration. Usually, if the number of records being processed is small and if there are few complex calculations, speed does not matter too much. When the number of records approaches a thousand, or there are several calculations per screen display, or there are long indexing operations, you will find that greater execution speed becomes essential.

The cost savings factor affects all dBASE users, not just those who develop applications for commercial sale. If you consider that any dBASE application which has a large number of users, for example one per supermarket outlet or one in every sub-office, will require a copy of a dBASE interpreter or a RunTime licence for each user, it becomes obvious that we are talking about large sums of money. By contrast, with a compiled application it costs little to distribute it to as many outlets or sub-offices as you wish.

Many developers will be interested in improvements to the language specification. The Clipper compiler has extended the dBASE specification so that you can relate up to 8 files at once, the number of memory variables has been extended into the thousands, and the maximum number of fields per database has increased to 1024. Also, by virtue of the fact that a compiled application can include linked routines, it is possible to build up libraries of external routines or programs that may be incorporated into the application. Chapter 4 describes the compilation and link steps in some detail, and explains how to use the DO or CALL commands to execute an external routine, while Chapter 6 describes how to create your own external functions.

Chapter Four
Compiling dBASE Programs

On many computers, particularly mainframe computers, the only way of executing a program is to compile it first. On personal computers we have been able to use languages like BASIC and dBASE which are interpretive, meaning that programs are executed in source form. The advantages of using a dBASE compiler have already been explained but you may, of course, take advantage of using both an interpreter and a compiler.

Let us, however, examine the possibility of not using an interpreter at all. It is perfectly feasible to use no more than a word processor to produce the source program and a compiler to produce the executable program. This approach is, after all, no different from that of COBOL or Pascal or C programmers who edit their source program, compile and link it, then execute it, and if it does not execute as intended they return to the edit stage and repeat the whole process. The drawback to this approach is that, in a simple development environment, one loses the value interpreters have in speeding up the development process.

Within an interpretive environment there are no delays between the editing process and the execution of the program. Moreover, if you are using a memory resident editor such as SideKick or WordStar's RUN command, you can flick between editor and interpreter at great speed. Not that dBASE II or dBASE III provide a great deal of assistance in getting to a problem source line: dBASE II simply shows you the source line without telling you where in your program it occurs, while dBASE III gives you the name of the particular .PRG file but does not provide a line number or any other means of knowing where in the .PRG file the line occurs. In this context a good example is set by the FoxBASE interpreter which provides both program filename and line number.

In a more sophisticated development environment where you are employing external functions not available within dBASE II or dBASE III, the value of developing with an interpreter may be less important. After all, if your application relies on features not available within dBASE II or dBASE III, you are not going to be able to test the application unless you compile it to include such extra features. A typical example of this is an application that depends on a SET RELATION situation covering more than just one parent/child relationship. If your application needs to relate three or four or more files in this way, then there is no point in attempting to test the application within dBASE III which does not recognise more than two such related files.

Let us look next at how to go about compiling a dBASE program, first in summary and then in more detail. The step of compiling a program is usually quite simple: you present the compiler with your program and it works through it producing the appropriate microprocessor instructions and converting the names of data items into memory addresses. From your .PRG files, it creates a machine code version of the program which it writes to a .OBJ file. The latter is read by the linker which produces an .EXE file containing your executable program. At the same time as translating your dBASE code into machine code, the compiler will be looking for errors, such as incorrect syntax. Any errors it finds will be displayed, giving you a chance to correct the source program before having another go at compiling it.

While looking at the process in more detail we will be using the Clipper compiler as an example. To execute the compiler from the DOS prompt you simply enter its name followed by the name of your dBASE program, for example:

```
clipper cars
```

If the dBASE program has sub-programs which are called and executed by DO commands, the sub-programs will automatically be included in the compilation process. The compilation will throw up any error which it discovers in your program, such as incorrect use of a command or incorrect pairing of DO...ENDDO, IF...ENDIF, and so on. Next an object or machine code file will be created which will have the same name as your dBASE program but with the filename extension .OBJ, for example CARS.OBJ.

This .OBJ file contains the microprocessor code that reflects your dBASE code. The .OBJ file is not, however, complete since the compile process relies on a second step, the link step, to pull in extra microprocessor code contained in other .OBJ files or, more typically, in a library of such files. The Link program has the means of combining a number of .OBJ files into a single library file that has a filename extension of .LIB. The extra microprocessor code will often be standard routines which perform input/output processing, or functions such as date conversion, or they may be your own specially written routines. If, for example, you expect to use a certain long-winded tax computation in more than one application program, you would probably be better off compiling it separately and using the dBASE CALL command to bring it into each application program as necessary. What this means is that you are relying on the Link program to find the machine code for the tax computation routine and bind it with the machine code of your application program to create a single executable program.

From the Link program's point of view, it is simply tying up loose ends: where it finds a reference to a routine that is not already part of the application program, it reads through specified .OBJ or library files trying to find the missing routines. All it asks of you is that you tell it the names of the appropriate object or library files and that you see to it that these files are ready to be read by the Link program. Included with the Clipper package is a library called CLIPPER.LIB which contains a large number of extra routines. Since many of the features available through the Clipper compiler are contained in the routines kept in the CLIPPER.LIB library, you will find that the first job of the Link program supplied with the Clipper compiler is to look for the CLIPPER.LIB file. The Link program is a version of Plink86 which has been specially adapted for use with Clipper. With other linkers, you have to tell the Link program the name of the library file, but this version of Plink86 automatically assumes that it needs to read CLIPPER.LIB. Thus to link your CARS program with Plink86, you simply enter the following against the DOS prompt:

```
plink86 fi cars
```

The FI is a keyword, short for FILE, which tells Plink86 that the next word is a filename. Many users employ a DOS batch file which contains the following:

```
clipper %1
plink86 fi %1
```

If the batch file is called CL.BAT, they would simply enter the following to execute both the compiler and the link program:

```
cl cars
```

To avoid Plink86 starting up in cases where Clipper found errors in the dBASE program, you can improve the batch file as follows:

```
clipper %1
if not errorlevel 1 plink86 fi %1
```

Clipper will set the DOS ERRORLEVEL to 1 if it finds an error during the compilation process, and then the batch IF statement will not allow Plink86 to be executed.

Where extra object or library files are required, such as those containing your own routines, you would add the name or names of these files to the PLINK86 line:

```
plink86 fi cars,taxlib
```

Each filename is separated by a comma from the previous filename. As explained above, the Link program will read through all the files you tell it to in order to resolve any missing references. You could therefore build up your own library of routines by compiling individual dBASE programs and combining them into a library using Plink86. The method of executing such routines from within a dBASE program can be performed by use of the CALL command, or by the DO command, or by using the name of the routine as a user defined function. Descriptions of these commands are given in Chapter 5 and user defined functions are explained at the end of Chapter 6.

At the end of the compile and link process we are left with an executable application in .EXE form that can be loaded directly into the memory of the computer to be executed. But what if the application is too large to fit into the available memory? You could, of course, increase the memory of your computer by adding a memory expansion card or extra memory chips. On the other hand, you may not want to impose this condition on your end users. And, in any case, the application will be too large only because the Link program has taken the code for each section of your application and laid it end to end one after the other, for example:

> MENU SECTION followed by
> APPEND RECORDS SECTION followed by
> CHANGE EXISTING RECORDS SECTION followed by
> SCREEN ENQUIRY SECTION followed by
> PRINTED REPORT SECTION.

Since you would be carrying out only one of these functions at any one time and therefore would not want more than the Menu Section plus one of the other sections at a time, it seems pointless having them all sitting in memory, needlessly taking up space. Far better to bring a section into memory as it is required by reading it from disk, much as the dBASE interpreters do when they encounter a DO command. The problem then is to explain to the Clipper compiler and the Link program that this is what you want to do.

Each section or group of sections that will be brought in from disk is called an *overlay*, so called because it overlays the previous section in the same area of memory. To overlay an application you must first of all decide which sections will become overlays. In our example it is quite straightforward; we decide to have four overlays consisting of the sections relating to the four menu options. Each overlay will follow the main Menu Section. Let us look at all the .PRG files in our application:

```
MENU SECTION                      CARS.PRG

APPEND RECORDS SECTION            CARS1.PRG

CHANGE EXISTING RECORDS SECTION   CARS2.PRG

SCREEN ENQUIRY SECTION            CARS3.PRG
                                  CARS31.PRG
                                  CARS32.PRG

PRINTED REPORT SECTION            CARS4.PRG
                                  CARS41.PRG
                                  CARS42.PRG
                                  CARS43.PRG
```

We are thus going to have CARS as our main program followed by four overlays:

```
CARS1

CARS2

CARS3 plus CARS31 plus CARS32

CARS4 plus CARS41 plus CARS42 plus CARS43
```

The size of the finished program will be that of the CARS section plus that of the largest overlay. In memory it will look like this:

CARS			
CARS1	CARS2	CARS3 CARS31 CARS32	CARS4 CARS41 CARS42 CARS43

As you can see, each overlay starts at the same memory location, i.e. immediately after the main menu program.

Now we have to find a way of explaining our overlaying plans to Clipper. Bear in mind that Clipper will normally attempt to include every .PRG file that is named by a DO command throughout the application. To prevent this happening so that we can present the Link program with separate sections of the application instead of a single large .OBJ file, we need to give Clipper a more specific instruction than we would normally. We want to ask it to create more than one .OBJ file and we want to be able to specify the contents of each .OBJ file. For example, in the first .OBJ file we want only the main Menu Section, i.e. CARS.PRG, not any of the sub-sections. In each of the other .OBJ files we want a complete sub-section, for example the final .OBJ file should represent the printed report section made up of CARS4.PRG, CARS41.PRG, CARS42.PRG, and CARS43.PRG.

The trick is really to stop Clipper from including program files that are not wanted in a particular .OBJ file. In the case of the sub-sections in our example this is not difficult because we can run the compiler once for each sub-section:

```
clipper cars1
clipper cars2
clipper cars3
clipper cars4
```

It does not matter that we have included sub-sections while compiling CARS3 and CARS4, since we do want those as part of their respective overlays. Having executed these four compilations, we now have four .OBJ files. We still have to compile the main Menu Section and prevent it from including the sub-sections we have already compiled. This is done by creating a special batch file containing the filenames of only those .PRG files that we want in the .OBJ file. This file will have a .CLP filename extension and will contain a line for each .PRG file in our selection. In the example, we need thus do no more than create a batch file called CARS.CLP containing the line CARS (the .PRG extension should not be supplied), and ask Clipper to compile it. The method of directing Clipper to a .CLP file is by adding an @ sign to the front of the filename. The example below will compile only the file contained in CARS.CLP instead of CARS.PRG together with all program files referenced by it:

```
clipper @cars
```

The .OBJ file will, of course, be called CARS.OBJ.

Now that we have five .OBJ files, we have to ask Plink86 to treat all but the first as mutually exclusive overlays. Here another batch file will come in useful: the .LNK file. What we will do is place all the commands for Plink86 in a .LNK file so that we can be confident of accurate input to the Link program. The first step is to indicate the name of the non-overlayed section, in this case CARS. This is done with the FILE (abbreviated to FI) keyword. Next we use the BEGINAREA (abbreviated to BEGIN) keyword to tell Plink86 that the overlays may start immediately after the previous section. This is followed with a line for each overlay. The line contains the keyword SECTION followed by the keyword FILE and the name of the appropriate .OBJ file. Finally, the end of overlaying is signalled by the keyword ENDAREA, abbreviated to END. Let us look at an example:

```
FI CARS
BEGIN
  SECTION FI CARS1
  SECTION FI CARS2
  SECTION FI CARS3
  SECTION FI CARS4
END
```

If you wanted to include routines contained in your own private library which you had called TAX.LIB, you would simply add an extra line:

```
FI CARS
LIB TAX
BEGIN
  SECTION FI CARS1
  SECTION FI CARS2
  SECTION FI CARS3
  SECTION FI CARS4
END
```

There is one other important consideration: all data items created within an overlay will normally be placed within the non-overlayed section, only the instruction code being placed in the overlay area. This might mean that in a large application program the main section becomes so large that even with overlaying it will not fit into the required memory. You may, however, specify otherwise by adding the following to your list of Plink86 commands:

```
OVERLAY NIL, $CONSTANTS
```

A complete example is shown below:

```
FI CARS
LIB TAX
OVERLAY NIL, $CONSTANTS
BEGIN
  SECTION FI CARS1
  SECTION FI CARS2
  SECTION FI CARS3
  SECTION FI CARS4
END
```

Another consideration is the use of procedure files. If you are calling procedures from more than one overlay, you cannot have the procedures in any of the overlays. The simplest way of overcoming this problem is to include the procedures in the main Menu Section which will always be in memory for use by any overlay. Remember that Clipper allows you to have your procedures at the foot of one of your existing .PRG files instead of separately in their own .PRG file. In our example you could thus add your procedures to CARS.PRG. If this causes memory size problems you will have to break up your procedures into smaller sections and include these in the overlay sections, even if it means duplicating some of the procedures.

This overview of using a Link program has been restricted to reasonably basic use, but you will find that the ability to link in external modules constitutes a very powerful addition to the dBASE language. You have at your command the means of calling up any software routine that will run on your personal computer, whether it has been written in Assembler, Pascal, Basic, C, or any other standard programming language including dBASE itself.

Chapter Five
The dBASE Commands

This book is not intended as a dBASE reference manual but as a guide to the use of the dBASE programming language. There are thus a small number of dBASE commands which are not covered in the descriptions of commands that follow. These are essentially full screen commands which were designed to make dBASE III more attractive when used interactively.

Obvious omissions in this book are the ASSIST and HELP commands, while others such as the commands concerned with Catalog files are mentioned only briefly. As a general rule, the emphasis is on the commands likely to be used within a program, although certain interactive commands dating from dBASE II days, such as CHANGE and BROWSE, are included in the descriptions. Also covered are full screen interactive commands which are used to set up files for other commands, for example CREATE REPORT or CREATE VIEW.

Other omissions include the product specific commands IMPORT and EXPORT which relate only to conversions from and to PFS files. Finally, there are a number of MODIFY commands which are exact duplicates of their CREATE counterparts, for example MODIFY LABEL and CREATE LABEL. In these cases, the MODIFY version has not been given its own entry but is mentioned under the CREATE equivalent.

Both the Clipper compiler and dBASE III PLUS contain commands that are not available in dBASE III versions earlier than dBASE III PLUS. If, in the descriptions that follow, it is stated that a command is a dBASE III PLUS command or a Clipper command, it means by implication that the command was not available in dBASE III versions earlier than dBASE III PLUS. It also means that, at the time of writing, it is not available in any of the other implementations of the language. Thus a command quoted as being Clipper only, is not available in dBASE III PLUS and vice versa. However, new software releases are issued so frequently that they tend to outdate books and, as regards implementations of the dBASE III specification, you should not be too concerned with distinctions made here. In the space of six months Ashton Tate have incorporated improvements to the language first seen in Clipper and the developers of Clipper have responded by incorporating other improvements first contained in dBASE III PLUS. Also, we should not lose sight of the fact that a new FoxBASE interpreter which is compatible with dBASE III PLUS (including multi-user features) has been announced, and may well be available by the time this book appears.

The descriptions of dBASE commands that follow are arranged alphabetically, but remember that this is not a reference section. It is instead a synopsis of the commands, showing differences between the dBASE II and dBASE III specifications, and pointing to implementation differences. It also contains cautions regarding pitfalls, and reminders of special techniques that you may care to use.

The ? or ?? command

Syntax: ? expression list
             ?? expression list

The ? command is used to display the contents of memory variables or database fields, the results of expressions, constants, or a mixture of these.

```
. ? make
Mercedes

. ? pageno
        6

. ? value*.9
    6852.600

. ? 366/2
183

. ? "USER ENQUIRY"
USER ENQUIRY

. ? model,pageno,value*.9,366/2
Mercedes          6     6852.600   183
```

When used to display a list of items, a single space will separate the result of each item:

```
. ? "Fred","Andrew"
Fred Andrew
```

The single space separator may be cancelled by issuing the SET RAW ON command (dBASE II specification only).

In the same way that the ? command can produce the result of a calculation, it can return the result of a function such as the system date, or of a logical expression:

```
. ? date()
12/12/85
```

```
. ? make = "BMW"
.T.
```

In the dBASE III specification, the ? command may be used to display the contents of a Memo field.

The results of the ? command will typically appear on the screen, but may be directed to the printer with the SET PRINT ON command. A ? command used on its own will display a blank line, so that the results of the next display will appear on the line below. For this reason, the ? command is often used to space down the screen or printed page. In a program it is possible to display a subsequent item on the same line by using a variation of this command, the ??:

```
? "Page "
?? str(pageno,2)
```

Other than the limited control afforded by the ? on its own and the ?? version of the command, the ? command cannot specify where on a screen the display will occur. For example, the only means of displaying an item to the right of the screen is to prefix it with the necessary amount of spacing:

```
? space(20),"ACCOUNTS LISTING"
```

If careful screen positioning is required, the @ SAY command should be used. The @ SAY command also has the means of formatting displayed fields with its PICTURE clauses, although this feature is now available to the ? and ?? commands in the latest dBASE III specification by means of the TRANSFORM function.

The @ BOX command

Syntax: @ top,left,bottom,right BOX character string

dBASE programmers frequently improve the appearance of a data entry or display screen by providing one or more boxes or frames to surround the data. For such programmers there are two commands available in the latest dBASE III specification. The dBASE III PLUS specification has the @ TO command, and the Clipper compiler the @ BOX command.

As its name implies the @ BOX command allows you to draw boxes on the screen. The size and relative position on the screen may be specified, and up to nine different characters may be employed in drawing a box. Four screen coordinates are supplied to indicate the positions of the corners of the box. The coordinates for top and bottom may be in the range 0 to 24, while the left and right sides may be in the range 0 to 79.

The character string supplied as part of the command dictates the characters that are to be used in drawing the box. The first character will be used to draw the top left corner, the second to draw the top line, the third to draw the top right corner, the fourth to draw the right side, and so forth in a clockwise direction.

If less than eight characters are supplied, the final one will be used to draw the remainder of the box. If a ninth character is supplied, it will be used to fill the box. To clear the box from the screen without disturbing the rest of the display, a null string may be used:

```
@ 5,5,25,75 box ""
```

Remember to enclose the character string in quotation marks. As an alternative, the character string may be placed in a memory variable and the name of the variable used in place of the string itself. This also means that special characters can be used in drawing the box, for example:

```
bchars1 = chr(201)+chr(205)+chr(187)+chr(186)
bchars2 = chr(188)+chr(205)+chr(200)+chr(186)
bchars  = bchars1+bchars2
@ 5,5,25,75 box bchars
```

The advantage of the @ BOX command or the @ TO command is that it provides in one command what one might otherwise achieve in ten or twenty, and it is very much faster than any alternative. There is no equivalent in the dBASE II specification or dBASE III versions earlier than dBASE III PLUS.

The @ PROMPT command

Syntax: @ row,col PROMPT character expression
               [MESSAGE character expression]

This is a Clipper compiler command which is used to place menu selections on the screen, and is intended to be used in conjunction with the MENU TO and SET MESSAGE TO commands, for example:

```
Set Message To 23
ə 21,11 Prompt ' Next '        Message ':- Display Next Record.'
ə 21,24 Prompt ' Previous '    Message ':- Display Previous Record.'
ə 21,40 Prompt ' Edit Memo '   Message ':- Edit The Text in The Box.'
ə 21,57 Prompt ' Quit '        Message ':- Leave Example Program.'
Menu To Menu1
*
Do Case
  Case (Menu1 = 0)  .OR. (Menu1 = 4)
    Close Data
    Quit
    *
  Case Menu1 = 1
    Skip
```

The string following the PROMPT keyword is displayed at the specified row,column coordinates, while the string following the Message keyword is displayed on the row specified in the SET MESSAGE TO command. The screen appearance of the example above would be as follows:

```
    Next           Previous        Edit Memo        Quit

 :- Display Next Record.
```

The MENU TO command will highlight the first prompt, at the same time displaying the associated message contained in the @ PROMPT command on the specified message line. If you move to the next prompt by means of the right arrow key, it will be highlighted and the message on the message line will change to that specified in the second @ PROMPT command.

A prompt, i.e. a menu option, may be selected by pressing the Return key, or either of the PgUp or PgDn keys. The MENU TO command is similar to the READ command in that the relative number of the selected prompt will be stored in the variable specified by the MENU TO command. A value of zero means that the Escape key has been pressed. The commands that follow the MENU TO command will be similar to those that follow a READ command in menu processing, for example the CASE command may be used to select an appropriate course of action depending on the prompt selected. Up to 32 prompts, i.e. 32 @ PROMPT command lines, may be given with a single MENU TO command. The prompts do not have to appear side by side as in the example: any of the usual row,column coordinates are acceptable.

The @ SAY GET command

dBASE II syntax:
    @ row,col   [SAY expression] [USING format]
                   [GET variable/fieldname] [PICTURE format]
dBASE III syntax:
    @ row,col   [SAY expression] [PICTURE format]
                   [GET variable/fieldname] [PICTURE format]
                   [RANGE expression, expression]
    @ row,col   [CLEAR]

In both the dBASE II and dBASE III specifications, the essential features of the @ SAY GET command may be seen in its ability to specify a particular position on the screen for either output or input, and to apply formatting rules to the display and input areas. The same is true of the @ SAY command for printed output. Let us look at these two aspects first.

On a screen the row coordinate can range from 0 for the leftmost position, to 79 for the rightmost position. The column coordinate can range from 0 for the top line of the screen to 23 for the bottom line of the screen. These values assume a screen of 24 times 80, and should be reinterpreted for a larger or smaller screen. Usually the top line, i.e. line 0 (and line 22 in dBASE III PLUS), is not used since it may be overwritten by status indications or messages (see the SET STATUS and SET SCOREBOARD commands). When applied to a printer, the maximum row or column coordinate must not exceed 255. In practice, however, the largest row is likely to be within the standard lines per page limit, for example 66 lines on 11 inch paper, and the largest column is likely to be a value such as 132 for condensed print on 80 column paper or standard print on 14.5 inch wide paper. If you decrease the row,column coordinate on printed output, a page throw is assumed. For example, if you issued @ 13,5 SAY "FRED" followed by @ 13,4 SAY "JACK", the latter will be interpreted as a request to throw to line 13 on a new page. On the screen such a sequence would simply display the second item at the coordinates requested, even if it means overwriting the previous item.

The expression in the @ SAY part of the command may be formatted. In the dBASE II specification this is done by means of the USING clause, while the dBASE III specification has PICTURE as the equivalent clause. In either case, certain special formatting characters (also known as a template) may be specified, for example the * may be used to replace leading zeros if you are printing cheques:

```
@ 12,60 say amount picture "***,***.99"
```

In place of an ***** we could have specified the $ sign to obtain a similar effect. The example above also shows the use of the full stop and comma as a means of separating the digits in a numeric value. Another formatting character is the exclamation mark ! which can be used to convert character strings to upper-case:

```
@ 12,60 say name picture "!!!!!!!!!!!!!"
```

Let us look at all the output formatting characters for both the dBASE II and dBASE III specifications:

Data type	dBASE II specification	dBASE III specification
Numeric	$ * # 9 ,	$ * # 9 ,
Character	! A X # 9	! A L X # 9
Logical		A L X # 9
Date		A L X # 9

Apart from the asterisk, dollar, exclamation mark and comma which have already been mentioned, these formatting characters may be used to display any character in the field or variable specified by the @ SAY command. If the field is numeric in type, the # and 9 will suppress leading zeros, i.e. the data fills up from the right of the formatting sequence. If the field is not numeric, the data fills up from the left. Let us look at an example of this:

```
store 123 to num
store "123" to char
@ 5,0 say num  picture "999,999"
@ 6,0 say num  picture "###,###"
@ 7,0 say char picture "999,999"


    123
    123
123
```

The L formatting character will display only the True or False status of the expression specified by the @ SAY command. Remember also that the formatting characters control the length of the display, for example:

```
@ 8,0 say "ABCDEF" picture "XXX"


ABC
```

In addition to the formatting characters or template, the dBASE III specification provides an extra formatting device in the form of a function. A formatting function consists of a single character prefixed by the @ sign, for example @E to obtain a European date format on just this one display:

```
ə 5,0 say today picture "əE"
```

The formatting functions are as follows:

@C : Displays CR after a positive value
@X : Displays DR after a negative value
@(: Encloses a negative value in parentheses
@B : Left justifies a value
@Z : Suppresses the display of a zero value
@D : Displays date in the form MM/DD/YY
@E : Displays date in the form DD/MM/YY
@A : Displays only alphabetic characters
@! : Converts lower-case to upper-case
@R : Sets on the insert mode so that characters other than the listed formatting characters will be inserted in the data instead of overwriting the data, i.e. a non-formatting character is treated just like the comma

Formatting characters and functions may be used in the same PICTURE clause provided they are separated by a space, for example:

```
ə 5,0 say num  picture "əB 999,999"
```

Just as the @ SAY expression may be formatted, you may format the @ GET expression. Most of the same formatting characters apply, though with a different interpretation. In the PICTURE clause of an @ GET command, the formatting characters control what the user may or may not enter into the field or variable. For example, the formatting character 9 will allow only digits, signs, a decimal point, or spaces. Let us look at the full set:

Data type	dBASE II specification	dBASE III specification
Numeric	# 9 ,	# 9 ,
Character	! A X # 9	! A L X # 9
Logical		L

The formatting functions that may be used with the @ GET command are as follows:

@B : Left justifies a value
@Z : Suppresses the display of a zero at the right of a numeric picture
@D : Accepts a date in the form MM/DD/YY
@E : Accepts a date in the form DD/MM/YY
@A : Accepts only alphabetic characters
@! : Converts lower-case to upper-case

@Sn : Limits the field width display to n characters but allows you to scroll from side to side within the specified width (this feature was introduced by dBASE III PLUS).

There are no date literals, which means that you have to create your own date variables by using the CTOD( ) function. To create an empty date variable for data entry, you could employ the following:

```
store ctod("  /  /  ") to datex
a 15,45 say "Please enter date " get datex
```

Another way of controlling the entry of numeric or date information is to use the RANGE clause which allows you to specify lower and upper limits, for example:

```
a 5,35 get num picture "999" range 101,499
```

If you try to enter a value of lower than 101 or higher than 499, a message will appear specifying the valid range and asking you to re-enter the item. You may specify only a lower limit or only an upper limit but the comma must be supplied:

```
a 5,35 get num picture "999" range 101,
```

If you want to specify a date range, you should again use the CTOD( ) function:

```
store ctod("  /  /  ") to datex
a 15,45 say "Please enter date " get datex ctod("01/01/86"),ctod("31/12/86")
```

Remember when using dates in this way to specify the date according to the current SET DATE format.

Note that the @ GET command does no more than display a data entry area on the screen, albeit containing the contents of the specified variable. To activate the cursor, and thus data entry, you have to issue the READ command.

The final syntax of the @ command is @ CLEAR, which provides a means of clearing the screen below and to the right of the coordinates, i.e. clearing a rectangle of the screen having its top left corner at the specified row,column coordinate and its bottom right corner at the bottom right of the screen.

@ SAY commands are not affected by the SET PRINT ON command. To obtain printed output you should first issue the SET FORMAT TO PRINT command (dBASE II specification) or the SET DEVICE TO PRINT command (dBASE III specification).

The @ **TO** command

Syntax: @ row,col [CLEAR] TO row,col [DOUBLE]

This dBASE III PLUS command is equivalent to the @ BOX command provided by the Clipper compiler. It will draw a box from the upper left row and column coordinate to the lower right row and column coordinate. The box will be drawn with a single line or, if the keyword DOUBLE is included, a double line. The command will also draw a single horizontal or vertical line if you use the same row or column coordinates respectively for upper left and lower right. The box may be cleared from the screen without disturbing the rest of the display by including the CLEAR keyword:

```
clear
@ 5,5 to 15,75 double
wait
@ 5,5 clear to 15,75
```

The ACCEPT command

Syntax: ACCEPT ['prompt'] TO variable

The ACCEPT command may be used as an alternative to the @ GET command to ask the user for character information (see also the INPUT command). The prompt is an optional character string which is valuable in explaining to the user what is being asked, for example:

```
accept "Please enter Make of Vehicle " to makex
```

Note the extra space at the end of the prompt. If this is not supplied, the user's response will begin immediately after the prompt, so that the screen could look like this:

```
Please enter Make of VehicleMercedes
```

It does not stop the program working, but it looks poor. In the dBASE II specification a colon is inserted to the right of the prompt.

It is important to remember that ACCEPT works on character data only and it does not need quote marks before and after the data. If you do supply the quote marks, they will be accepted as part of the data. Also, you do not need to initialise a variable in order to use it in the ACCEPT command. Indeed, ACCEPT will change the type of a variable from its previous status, for example numeric, to that of character. Let us look at an illustration of this:

```
store 2 to char1
accept "Please enter Make " to char1
accept "Please enter Model " to char2
display memory
wait
```

In this program, which sets up one numeric variable but does not initialise the second, ACCEPT nevertheless results in the following:

```
Please enter Make BMW
Please enter Model 320i
CHAR1        priv  C  "BMW"
CHAR2        priv  C  "320i"
    2 variables defined,       11 bytes used
Press any key to continue.....
```

Note that the ACCEPT command is self-contained; it does not have to be followed by a READ command as does the @ GET command. With ACCEPT, as soon as the Return key is pressed the user's entry is passed to the program. The drawback to this command is that you cannot format the entry field in the way that the @ GET command does with the PICTURE clause.

Another point to look out for is that it is possible to generate a null variable in dBASE III or Clipper if the user simply presses the Return key without entering any data. The way to test for a null variable is to use the LEN function which will give a zero length in such circumstances. The same situation in dBASE II will result in a single space character.

The && command

Syntax: && text

The && command is a variation on the NOTE or * command. It allows you to place comments in your program on lines already occupied by other commands. Mention has already been made in Chapter 2 of providing explanatory comments on command lines such as ENDDO and ENDIF. The && command takes this a step further by letting you place comments on any line:

```
if reply = 'Y'      && Test if Printer switched on
```

The && command is not available in the dBASE II specification, or in dBASE III versions earlier than dBASE III PLUS.

The APPEND command

Syntax: APPEND [BLANK]
APPEND FROM filename [SDF] [DELIMITED]
[FOR/WHILE condition]

The APPEND command may be used in several ways as the different syntaxes given above indicate. All of these, however, result in the addition of a record or records physically to the end of the .DBF file currently in USE. There may be an index in operation which will give the impression that the appended records have somehow been inserted into a logical sequence, but in practice the APPEND command always adds new records at the end of the database file. It does, of course, update any indexes (if these are specified at the time) to reflect the logical sequence of the records which have been added.

The APPEND command on its own takes the user into interactive mode. This means that the fields of the database file currently in USE in the active work area are displayed on the screen, awaiting the entry of data. At the end of each set of fields, i.e. when the user has entered the last field in sequence, a record containing the entered information is added to the database file and another empty screen appears ready for the next record. The simplest method of exiting from the APPEND mode is by pressing the Return key on the very first character of an empty data entry screen.

In the dBASE III specification it is possible to go to an earlier record, i.e. into EDIT mode, by using the PgUp or CTRL and R key combination. While in EDIT mode, you can use the PgUp and PgDn keys to move backwards and forwards through the records. Bear in mind that the sequence of going from one record to another is dictated by the controlling index, or if no indexes are in operation, by the physical sequence of the records. The APPEND mode resumes when you return forward (with the PgDn or CTRL and C key combination) to the current record.

In Clipper, as with other interactive commands such as EDIT, APPEND on its own is not supported. When writing programs, whether using one of the dBASE interpreters or not, you would use the APPEND BLANK command. This command performs an addition to the database file by creating an empty or blank record, after which you would use the REPLACE or READ command to fill the empty fields of that record. A typical sequence looks like this:

```
set bell off
set intensity on
set talk off
use names index names
store .Y. to continue
store "      " to catx
store 0 to added
do while continue
   store space(50) to namex
   store namex to addr1x,addr2x,addr3x,addr4x,addr5x,addr6x
   store space(15) to telnox
   store space(30) to idx
   clear
   a 1,0 say "ADD A NAME"
   a  5,0 say "Name        " get namex
   a  7,0 say "Address     " get addr1x
   a  8,0 say "            " get addr2x
   a  9,0 say "            " get addr3x
   a 10,0 say "            " get addr4x
   a 11,0 say "            " get addr5x
   a 12,0 say "            " get addr6x
   a 14,0 say "Telephone   " get telnox
   a 16,0 say "Surname/Ident " get idx ;
       pict "!!!!!!!!!!!!!!!!!!!!!!!!!!!!!!!!"
   a 18,0 say "Category     " get catx pict "!!!!!!"
   read
   if namex = "  "
     store .F. to continue
   else
      a 23,0 say "Please wait for a moment ....."
      append blank
      replace name with namex
      replace addr1 with addr1x,addr2 with addr2x
      replace addr3 with addr3x,addr4 with addr4x
      replace addr5 with addr5x,addr6 with addr6x
      replace telno with telnox,id with idx,cat with catx
      store added +1 to added
   endif
enddo
return
```

The APPEND FROM command is used to add records to the database file currently in USE from either another database file or from an external file in standard ASCII format. The FOR or WHILE clauses operate much as they do in the description given with the DISPLAY command, i.e. they control the conditions under which records will be added to the .DBF file currently in USE. When neither SDF nor

DELIMITED is specified, the FROM file is expected to be another .DBF file. During the APPEND operation, a matching exercise occurs whereby fields with the same names and types are taken, on a record by record basis, from the FROM file and added to the file in USE. Too long fields are truncated while short fields are padded out with extra characters. Fields in the database file currently in USE which do not have a match in the FROM database will be left unused.

The SDF and DELIMITED clauses are used when you want to import data from a file other than a .DBF database. The possibilities include a file created from a spreadsheet such as SuperCalc or a file called down from a mainframe computer. In all cases, such files are expected to be standard ASCII text files. Unless otherwise specified, the filename of such a file will be expected to have a .TXT extension.

SDF stands for System Data Format and simply means that the text will consist of a series of unbroken characters representing the information to be passed over. Each 'record' will be terminated by the standard ANSI end of line characters (hexadecimal 0D0A). Also, both numeric and character information will appear in character format. Indeed dBASE will be unable to make any sense of what it can only view as a long string of characters. It succeeds in transferring the information only because it allocates characters to .DBF fields according to the size of the .DBF fields. If the latter conform to what appears in the external file, the transfer will be successful. You can use the EDIT command to have a look at the first record to see whether the fields look as you expect. If they do not, you simply modify the structure of the database file slightly and try again. By the way, while you are experimenting it is not necessary to complete the APPEND operation each time. After a few records, you can press the Escape key to stop the operation.

One very rewarding use to which this approach can be put is to receive data from a mainframe computer in print form, i.e. exactly as it would appear if it were printed on a line printer attached to the mainframe. The trick, then, is to adapt the structure of the receiving .DBF file to conform to the layout of the individual print lines. Once that has been done, APPEND FROM SDF will copy the mainframe data into the database as explained above. You will now have a database containing print lines, but with data items properly defined as fields. Afterwards, you can create a copy of this database using the FIELDS clause to select only those items you want and ignore the blank spaces between fields. You will also want to delete records representing print lines that do not contain information, for example spacing lines or page heading lines. Of course, the whole process can be made much simpler by having a mainframe program that writes the details exactly as you would want them for your database file.

The DELIMITED clause has a more specific use than the SDF clause, although it operates in much the same way. It assumes that the data will be in a form whereby the fields are separated by commas and character fields enclosed by a delimiter such as quote marks. Typically this means that the data is from an ASCII file that has been created by spreadsheet software. The data will still appear in character form but the presence of the delimiters makes the APPEND job much simpler. All dBASE has to do is take each group of characters between two delimiters, and assign it to the .DBF fields in sequence. Let us look at a short example:

```
"BMW","320i","Jones"
```

The above would correspond to the first three fields of the database file irrespective of length:

```
1  MAKE       Character      10
2  MODEL      Character       8
3  USER       Character      17
```

If the alphabetic fields are enclosed by a character other than quote marks, you can add the WITH clause to specify this delimiter. Fields will be written to database fields according to their sequence, i.e. the first field will be written to the first database field, the second field to the second database field, and so forth. The quote marks or alternative delimiter will, of course, be stripped.

There are several packages which provide facilities for creating external files which are text copies of data held in an internal format, for example the SuperCalc spreadsheet software. Typically the fields in such text files are separated by commas and may thus be read by dBASE III. dBASE III PLUS has enhanced this feature by allowing you to append directly from certain spreadsheet formats. It has added three more clauses that may be used in place of the SDF clause:

- WKS to append from Lotus 1-2-3 spreadsheet format files, i.e. .WKS files
- SYLK to append from Multiplan spreadsheet format files
- DIF to append from VisiCalc format files.

The AVERAGE command

Syntax: AVERAGE field list [scope] TO memory variable list
[FOR/WHILE condition]

The purpose of this command is to provide an arithmetic mean of one or more fields in the database currently in USE. The command does not exist in the dBASE II specification.

In dBASE III the command may be used interactively, i.e. without supplying the names of memory variables which are to receive the result(s) of the command. In a dBASE program (and thus also in Clipper) the memory variables are necessary, since without these you could not use the result(s). In either case, if memory variables are used it follows that there must be one variable for each field.

The SCOPE clause allows you to limit the command, for example by specifying the NEXT one or more records. The FOR/WHILE clauses allow you to impose conditions on the records to be processed in the course of the AVERAGE command. A typical use of the conditional clause would be as follows:

```
store "BMW" to makex
average miles to milesx for make = makex
? makex," : Average miles per vehicle = ",milesx
```

By its nature, the AVERAGE command implies that its usage is restricted to numeric fields only. An error will result if you try to specify a non-numeric field. Note too that the AVERAGE command reads through the database file and will thus change the current record number.

The BROWSE command

Syntax: BROWSE [FIELDS field list] [NOFOLLOW]

BROWSE is an interactive command that is available in both the dBASE II and dBASE III specifications, although it is not supported by the Clipper compiler. It is a look and change command that should be used with great care since even inadvertent changes will be written to the database file.

The BROWSE command displays the fields of each record across the screen, one record per line. If the fields of the record will not all fit into the width of the screen, as many complete fields as can be contained in the screen width will be shown. A number of records will be shown at a time and you may use the standard cursor control keys to move about on the screen making changes as you go.

Other editing controls such as CTRL and G to delete or CTRL and V to set insert mode on or off may also be used. To get at the fields that do not fit into a screen width, you use the CTRL and B or CTRL and right arrow keys to move the records, a field at a time, to the left. The screen acts as a window on the records and as one field leaves the screen at the left, the right-hand side of the screen fills with more fields. To pan the screen left, i.e. move the records to the right, you use the CTRL and Z or CTRL and left arrow keys. To move left and right a field at a time within a screen you use the CTRL and A and CTRL and F cursor control keys respectively. If you do not need all your fields on the screen you can add the FIELDS clause which allows you to specify only the fields you want to see on the screen.

dBASE III PLUS has extended the syntax of the BROWSE command, mainly by adding into the syntax options previously available interactively in dBASE III, such as FREEZE and LOCK. However, since this book is more concerned with dBASE programming than interactive use, you are referred to my book on dBASE III itself; *dBASE III: A Practical Guide*, published by Collins. The one dBASE III PLUS addition to the syntax that does deserve mention is the NOFOLLOW clause. This, when used while you are working in indexed sequence, enables you to retain your position in the file even when you change the contents of an indexed field. The current record pointer will be set to the record that previously followed the one you have just changed, i.e. the one that would have been next before you made the change.

The CALL command

dBASE III Syntax:
   CALL module name [WITH character expression/memory variable]
Clipper Syntax:
   CALL module name [WITH parameter list]

The CALL command in dBASE III PLUS executes an external program or routine placed in memory by the LOAD command. The filename of the binary file specified by the LOAD command becomes the module name to be specified in the CALL command, except for the filename extension which should not be included.

The WITH clause allows you to pass a parameter to the called module, either as a character string or by giving the name of a variable that contains the value to be passed. The variable can be of any type. When you no longer need the module in memory, you can remove it by means of the RELEASE MODULE command.

In Clipper, the CALL command will pass control to a module which has been compiled or assembled separately and then linked in with your dBASE program. Such modules must conform to the calling and parameter passing conventions employed by Clipper, namely those of the C language, and they must be in a format that conforms to the requirements of the linker, Plink86. In object module form they may either be held as .OBJ files or they may be contained in a .LIB library file.

Up to seven parameters may be passed to the called routine. All parameters are passed by reference, i.e. as pointers, which means that the called routine should be careful not to overwrite adjacent data items by increasing the length of a data item. Character strings are terminated by a null, i.e. a 0 byte at the end of the string. Numeric data items are passed in eight byte floating point form, but you may use the WORD( ) function to convert these from DOUBLE to type INT.

The CANCEL command

Syntax: CANCEL

The CANCEL command, as its name indicates, cancels execution of the dBASE program and returns control to the software that initiated the dBASE program. In the case of dBASE II, dBASE III, or FoxBASE, this will be the interpreter itself, i.e. to the dot prompt. The program file will be closed but all other files left open, including any procedure files that may have been opened. In the case of a compiled program, i.e. a stand alone .EXE program, control will be returned to the operating system. In this instance all open files will be closed exactly as they are in the QUIT command.

The CHANGE command

Syntax: CHANGE [scope] [FIELDS field list] [FOR/WHILE condition]

CHANGE is an interactive command that is available in both dBASE II and dBASE III specifications, although not in Clipper. It is used interactively to provide full screen editing of selected records and fields of the database file currently in USE.

It is effectively a way of editing database records without looking at every record in turn. This command is a cross between the EDIT and the REPLACE commands. If, for example, you wanted to examine and possibly change the commission rates of all salesmen in the South East sales area, you would not want to edit the records individually, only those for the South East:

```
. change for area = "SE" fields commission,name
```

After you have entered the above the screen will clear and the first record that meets the condition will be displayed on the screen just as for the EDIT command, but with the difference that only the fields specified by the FIELDS clause will appear. The NAME field is included not for editing purposes but so that there is some means of identifying the record being displayed.

Note that the fields are specified in the sequence that you want to see them on the screen. If you do not use the FIELDS clause, all the fields will be displayed just with in the EDIT command.

The CLEAR command

Syntax: CLEAR [ALL] [GETS] [MEMORY] [FIELDS]

The CLEAR command on its own suffers somewhat from two very different interpretations in the dBASE II and dBASE III specifications. In the former it is a command to be approached with caution since it resets or closes all dBASE files, including the .DBF file currently in USE. In dBASE III it performs the job of the dBASE II ERASE command, i.e. all it does is clear the screen. Given the possible confusion, let us separate the interpretations.

dBASE II specification

CLEAR on its own closes all database files, releases all memory variables, and re-selects the PRIMARY work area. The equivalent in the dBASE III specification is the CLEAR ALL command.

The CLEAR GETS command is a valuable, if not essential, method of clearing all the GETS issued in the course of a group of @ GET commands. Each @ GET occupies working space within the dBASE program, and since a maximum of 64 @ GETs are allowed, it may become important to release these.

Another use to which the CLEAR GETS command may be put is to ask the user to re-enter an item which has not passed a validation test. The CLEAR GETS command will leave the screen intact, showing all the previously entered details, but by issuing a new @ GET the cursor will be positioned at the field which is to be re-entered.

The ALL, MEMORY, and FIELDS clauses do not form part of the dBASE II syntax. CLEAR ALL is the same as CLEAR in dBASE II, while CLEAR MEMORY is the same as RELEASE ALL.

dBASE III specification

The CLEAR command on its own clears the screen of any previously displayed data and positions the cursor at the top left corner of the screen, i.e. at position 0,0. At the same time, any @ GETS still in effect are cleared

The CLEAR GETS command operates as it does in dBASE II, except that it is less important as regards the need to release @ GETS, since dBASE III allows 128 @ GETS.

The CLEAR MEMORY command is equivalent to the RELEASE ALL command. It releases all memory variables so that any information which has been stored in variables will no longer be available. There is, however, less urgency in controlling memory variables with dBASE III and Clipper. Whereas dBASE II allows a maximum of only 64 memory variables, dBASE III permits 256 and Clipper several thousand.

The CLEAR ALL command is equivalent to CLEAR on its own in dBASE II. It closes all database files including the one currently in USE, closes indexes and other open files, releases all memory variables, and re-selects work area 1.

The CLEAR FIELDS command releases all fields previously selected by the SET FIELDS TO command. Note that they will be released in all work areas, not just the currently selected work area.

The CLEAR TYPEAHEAD command

Syntax: CLEAR TYPEAHEAD

The dBASE III specification includes a typeahead buffer for keyboard input. This means that when you issue a command such as WAIT TO, it is possible that dBASE might read a character already present in the buffer rather than one entered in response to the WAIT prompt. CLEAR TYPEAHEAD is a dBASE III PLUS command that allows you to guard against any spurious characters that may have been left in the keyboard typeahead buffer by clearing the buffer. If you want to disable the typeahead buffer you can do so with the SET TYPEAHEAD command by specifying a buffer size of zero, but this will not work if you have issued the SET ESCAPE OFF command. At the time of writing, CLEAR TYPEAHEAD was to be found only in dBASE III PLUS. The equivalent command with the Clipper compiler is KEYBOARD.

The CLOSE command

Syntax: CLOSE file type
  CLOSE ALL

The CLOSE command may be seen as a refinement of the CLEAR ALL command which, in addition to closing files, will release all active memory variables. CLOSE also allows you to close files more discriminately, for example format files only. The file type may be one of the following:

```
ALTERNATE
DATABASES
FORMAT
INDEX
PROCEDURE
```

CLOSE DATABASES will close all open database, index, and format files. If you want to close just those in the currently selected work area, you should issue the USE command instead. CLOSE INDEX and CLOSE FORMAT apply only to the currently selected work area. CLOSE ALL will close every open file irrespective of type. Used on its own in Clipper, CLOSE will close down the .DBF and associated indexes currently in USE in the currently selected work area. dBASE III does not permit the use of CLOSE on its own. The dBASE II specification does not include the CLOSE command.

The CONTINUE command

Syntax: CONTINUE

The purpose of this command is to continue to search the database file for a record that matches the condition specified in the FOR clause of the previous LOCATE command. The search starts at the record following the current record: it is as if the LOCATE command had been reissued with a different starting point.

As soon as a record is found which satisfies the specified conditions, the operation stops. As with LOCATE, this record will now be the current record, which means that any of the commands such as DISPLAY or REPLACE, which act on the current record, may be used next.

The results of an unsuccessful match will be the same as for LOCATE, i.e. if a record matching the specified conditions is not found the current record will be the last record in the file and the end of file condition will be set. However, if a scope clause such as NEXT has been employed, the current record after an unsuccessful LOCATE will be the last record included in the scope clause.

The COPY command

Syntax: COPY TO filename [scope] [FIELDS field list]
[FOR/WHILE condition] [SDF] [DELIMITED]

On its own, the COPY command will create a duplicate of the database file in USE. The FIELDS clause may be used to limit the COPY so that only the named fields are included in the new database file. The fieldnames of the fields to be included should be separated by commas. Note that the dBASE II syntax specifies the singular FIELD while the dBASE III syntax specifies plural FIELDS. Either is acceptable since with the dBASE language only the first four characters are important. In the dBASE III specification, an associated .DBT file (which contains the text relating to Memo fields) will automatically be copied as part of the process of copying the .DBF file.

The SCOPE clause allows you to limit the command, for example by specifying the NEXT one or more records. The FOR/WHILE clauses allow you to impose conditions on the records to be processed in the course of the COPY command, for example to copy only records representing vehicles purchased within the most recent two years. The SET DELETED ON/OFF command may be used respectively to ignore or include records which have had the deleted marker set (see DELETE command).

The SDF clause provides the means of copying some or all of a database to an external file which will be in standard ASCII format and thus accessible to other programs. All the other COPY command keywords (except DELIMITED) are available, such as FOR, WHILE, and so forth. The reason for this feature is that the data in a dBASE database file cannot readily be accessed by other programs such as a word processor, or spreadsheet, or even a programming language like BASIC or COBOL. By using the SDF clause, the data is written out in a standard text format.

The file will be created with the same filename but with a .TXT file extension. You may instead specify the full filename if you would prefer a different file extension. Each record on this file will be as long as the database record itself, not counting the extra deletion marker character used by dBASE itself. The details will appear much as they would if you were to show them with the LIST command but without a record number or separating spaces between fields.

The problem with this format is that an external program would not know where a field starts or ends since it would see the record simply as a long string of characters. This may be overcome by using the clause DELIMITED instead of SDF. This time the fields will be separated by commas and the alphabetic fields enclosed in quote marks. You may specify that alphabetic fields are enclosed not by quotes but with a character of your own choice by adding the WITH clause. The latter is simply added to the DELIMITED clause together with your choice of delimiter. For example DELIMITED WITH / will result in /BMW/ rather than 'BMW'. Empty alphabetic fields will be indicated only by the presence of a pair of quote marks or a pair of the characters specified in the WITH clause. Empty numeric fields will contain a zero value.

There are several packages which provide facilities for reading external files which are text copies of data held in dBASE format, for example the spreadsheet program SuperCalc. They usually expect the fields in such text files to be separated by commas, and provide the means of reading in the external file and transferring its contents to a spreadsheet. dBASE III PLUS has enhanced this feature by adding three more clauses that may be used in place of the SDF clause:

- WKS to create Lotus 1-2-3 spreadsheet format files, i.e. .WKS files
- SYLK to create Multiplan spreadsheet format files
- DIF to create VisiCalc format files.

The COPY FILE command

Syntax: COPY FILE filename TO filename

In contrast to the COPY command which will copy only the current database file, the COPY FILE command will copy any file, performing much the same function as the DOS COPY command. Note that it is necessary to supply the full filename including the extension. Remember too, if you are copying a database file, that there may be a .DBT file containing associated Memo fields and that this file should also be copied. An open file, for example a database file in USE, cannot be copied.

The COPY FILE command does not exist in the dBASE II specification. You may copy a database file that is in USE by means of the COPY TO command but not other files. In the dBASE III specification you may, if there is enough memory to do so, use the RUN command to execute the DOS COPY command as an alternative to the dBASE COPY FILE command. The reason for mentioning this is that the COPY FILE command does not permit the use of a skeleton such as *.DBF.

The COPY STRUCTURE command

Syntax: COPY STRUCTURE [EXTENDED] TO filename [FIELDS field list]

The COPY STRUCTURE command will copy the structure of the
database file in USE. The resulting file will be identical but empty of
data. The new structure may, of course, be changed with the MODIFY
STRUCTURE command. In the dBASE III specification the associated
.DBT memo file will also be copied, but the copy will, also, be empty.

The FIELDS clause may be used to limit the COPY STRUCTURE
so that only the named fields are included in the new structure. The
fieldnames of the fields to be included should be separated by commas.

The EXTENDED clause is used when you want to create an extended
structure which may subsequently be used with the CREATE FROM
command to create a new database file:

```
. use motor
. list stru
Structure for database : C:motor.dbf
Number of data records :        1
Date of last update     : 11/14/86
Field  Field name  Type        Width     Dec
    1  MAKE        Character     10
    2  MODEL       Character      8
    3  USER        Character     17
    4  VALUE       Numeric        9       2
    5  YEAR        Numeric        2
    6  NOTES       Memo          10
    7  MILES       Numeric        5
    8  LASTDATE    Date           8
** Total **                      70

. copy structure extended to motor99
```

The structure of the TO file will look like this:

```
Field  Field name  Type        Width     Dec
    1  FIELD_NAME  Character     10
    2  FIELD_TYPE  Character      1
    3  FIELD_LEN   Numeric        3
    4  FIELD_DEC   Numeric        3
** Total **                      18
```

Each record within this database will contain the details of one field, for
example:

```
. list
Record    FIELD_NAME FIELD_TYPE FIELD_LEN FIELD_DEC
     1    MAKE       C              10         0
     2    MODEL      C               8         0
     3    USER       C              17         0
     4    VALUE      N               9         2
     5    YEAR       N               2         0
     6    NOTES      M              10         0
     7    MILES      N               5         0
     8    LASTDATE   D               8         0
```

You can now change the contents of these records, by using the REPLACE command, so that the fields are named and defined as it suits you.

The EXTENDED clause applies to both the dBASE II and dBASE III specifications, but you cannot use it in conjunction with the FIELDS clause. In dBASE II the FIELDS clause will be ignored and all of the fields in the database in USE will be written as data records to the new file, while dBASE III regards the combination of EXTENDED and FIELDS clauses as a syntax error. If you do want to limit the fields, you could afterwards delete the records corresponding to the unwanted fields. See the CREATE command for more details on the EXTENDED clause.

The COUNT command

Syntax: COUNT [scope] TO memory variable [FOR/WHILE
            condition]

This command provides a count or tally either of the total number of records in the database file currently in USE, or only of those records which meet the specified condition(s). In the interpreters like dBASE II, FoxBASE, and dBASE III, the command may be used interactively, i.e. without supplying the names of memory variables which are to receive the result(s) of the command. In a dBASE program the memory variables are necessary since without these you could not use the result(s).

The SCOPE clause allows you to limit the command, for example by specifying the NEXT one or more records. The FOR/WHILE clauses allow you to impose conditions on the records to be processed in the course of the COUNT command. A typical use of the conditional clause would be as follows:

```
store "BMW" to makex
count to carsx for make = makex
? makex," : Total Number of Vehicles = ",carsx
```

Bear in mind that an interactive command such as COUNT, unless it is limited by the SCOPE clause, will read through the entire database file to perform its task. In most instances, this would be an unacceptable method of arriving at a tally since the operation prevents any other processing. For example, you cannot list and count the records at the same time. Usually it is not much more work, and is far more economical, to maintain your own count in a memory variable as you work your way through the database file.

The CREATE command

Syntax: CREATE [filename] [FROM filename]

The CREATE command is used to create a new .DBF database file. If the filename is not specified you will be asked for a filename. Next, you will be asked to supply the following for each field of the database:

```
Name
Type
Width
Number of Decimal Places
```

The name may be up to ten characters in length. The type may be character, numeric, or logical. In the dBASE III specification two more types are allowed: date and memo.

Character fields are used to contain text but may just as comfortably be used to contain digits, for example file numbers or telephone numbers. A field is usually defined as numeric if you need to total it or if you intend to perform arithmetic on its contents, such as a number of units or money. A numeric field with decimals has to be large enough to include the decimal point. For example, a numeric field with a width of 8 and 2 decimals will take a maximum value of 99999.99 since the decimal point takes up one of the 8 positions. Indeed, if you want to be able to hold negative amounts you also have to allow an extra position for the minus sign. Thus -83.75 would occupy 6 positions, defined as 6,2.

A logical field is always one character in size and is used as an indicator, i.e. it contains Y or N for yes or no, or T or F for true or false. A date field is always 8 characters in size and is actually stored as the number of days since 1 January 1901 (to allow you to perform easy date arithmetic) although it always appears in usual date form, as MM/DD/YY or DD/MM/YY (see SET DATE BRITISH). A Memo field occupies 10 characters in the database record but it allows you to keep up to 4096 characters of text in an associated file.

The CREATE command we have discussed so far is used interactively. If you need to create a .DBF database file non-interactively, i.e. from within a program, you would use the FROM clause. To do so, it will be necessary to have an extended structure (see the COPY STRUCTURE EXTENDED command). This means that the FROM file will have a structure which looks like this:

```
Field  Field name  Type       Width   Dec
    1  FIELD_NAME  Character     10
    2  FIELD_TYPE  Character      1
    3  FIELD_LEN   Numeric        3
    4  FIELD_DEC   Numeric        3
** Total **                     18
```

Each record within this database will contain the details of one field, for example:

```
. list
Record   FIELD_NAME FIELD_TYPE FIELD_LEN FIELD_DEC
     1   MAKE       C             10          0
     2   MODEL      C              8          0
     3   USER       C             17          0
     4   VALUE      N              9          2
     5   YEAR       N              2          0
     6   NOTES      M             10          0
     7   MILES      N              5          0
     8   LASTDATE   D              8          0
```

As you can see, it is a simple matter to change the contents of these records from within a program (by using the REPLACE command) so that the fields are named and defined as it suits us. After that the CREATE FROM command will take care of the rest. In some versions of dBASE II it is also possible to CREATE FROM an ordinary .DBF database file but this is really only the COPY STRUCTURE command in a different guise.

In the Clipper compiler, since there are no interactive commands, a separate utility takes the place of the CREATE command. There is, however, the CREATE FROM command which works exactly as explained above. Clipper also has an extra CREATE command which will create an empty extended structure, i.e. it performs the same function as the COPY STRUCTURE EXTENDED command but with no records in the extended database. The syntax of this CREATE command is identical to the standard command:

```
CREATE filename
```

The CREATE utility supplied as a stand alone program with the Clipper compiler may be used to create or to modify a database file. It is very similar in usage to the CREATE command, and the database file it creates can also be used by programs running interpretively under dBASE III.

The CREATE LABEL command

Syntax: CREATE LABEL filename
              MODIFY LABEL filename

The CREATE LABEL command is used to create a new label format file for use by the LABEL command. It does not exist in dBASE II, and in Clipper the function is supplied as a separate utility. Label formats created by the Clipper utility (which is called LABEL) may be used within dBASE III itself.

The details that may be specified in either the CREATE LABEL command or Clipper's LABEL utility are as follows:

Width of label :	35
Height of label :	5
Left Margin :	0
Lines between labels :	1
Spaces between labels :	0
Number of labels across :	1

The values shown above are preset to save you time but you may, of course, change them to suit your own requirements. Having specified the appearance of the label, you would next supply the content of each label. There will be as many lines as you have asked for, five if we accept the preset value shown above, for example:

```
title,inits,surname
addr1
addr2
addr3
addr4
```

You do not have to concern yourself with the positioning of fields on the same line because the CREATE LABEL command will automatically TRIM fields that are separated by commas. The first line above will be treated as if it had been entered as:

```
trim(title)+' '+trim(inits)+' '+surname
```

You can use only character fields in a label but functions like STR may, of course, be used to convert numeric data into character form.

When you have created the label format, the details will be written to a file with the filename you specified plus the extension .LBL, for example NAMES.LBL. If subsequently you want to modify the report details you can either issue the same CREATE LABEL command again or use the MODIFY LABEL command; the two are identical. With Clipper, the LABEL utility is similarly used to create or modify. The screens will appear exactly as before but they will contain all the details you entered previously.

The CREATE QUERY command

Syntax: CREATE QUERY filename
           MODIFY QUERY filename

CREATE QUERY is a command of dBASE III PLUS only, used to create a .QRY query file for use by the SET FILTER TO command. The latter allows you to specify a condition which will filter the database file so that only records that meet the condition appear to exist. The condition may be any simple test such as MAKE = 'BMW' or a combination of tests. The details that may be specified in the CREATE QUERY command are as follows:

- Fieldnames, for example MAKE
- Operators, for example EQUAL TO
- Constants or expressions, for example 'BMW'
- Connectors, for example .AND.

As you can see from the presence of connectors, the condition may be a complex one involving several operators. The details may subsequently be modified by means of the MODIFY QUERY command.

The CREATE REPORT command

Syntax: CREATE REPORT filename
           MODIFY REPORT filename

The CREATE REPORT command is used to create a new report format file for use by the REPORT command. It does not .exist in dBASE II since there the REPORT command itself is used to create new REPORT formats. In Clipper the function is supplied as a separate utility. Report formats created by the Clipper utility (which is called REPORT) may be used within dBASE III itself.

If you do not provide the report filename, you will be asked for one. The CREATE REPORT command is a full screen interactive command that proceeds through a series of screens or windows (the latter in dBASE III PLUS) which allow you to specify the appearance and contents of your report. If we use dBASE III PLUS as an example, the first window allows you to enter the following details:

Report title or heading
Page width in characters   80
Left margin   8
Right margin   0
Lines per page   58
Double space report   No
Page eject before printing   Yes
Page eject after printing   No
Plain page   No

The report heading will be centralised within the page width and will be printed on every page of the report. Four lines, each sixty characters long may be used for the heading. The rest of the options shown above relate to the page characteristics. Each option will have a preset value as indicated above but you may, of course, change the values. The 'Page eject before printing' option refers to whether or not your report should cause the printer to advance a page before beginning the report. Similarly, the 'Page eject after printing' refers to what should happen when the last line of the report has been printed. The 'Plain page' option specifies whether the report should appear without page numbers and system date, and with the report heading on the first page only.

When you have completed these details, the next window will ask you for information concerning sub-totals:

Group on expression
Group heading
Summary report only
Page eject after group
Sub-group on expression
Sub-group heading

If you do not want sub-totalling, you simply move on to the next window. Otherwise you enter the 'Group on expression', which is usually the fieldname that will control the sub-totalling so that whenever the contents of this field change, for example at the end of all the records for the South East sales area, a sub-total may be printed. You may also specify that you want to see only the sub-totals and not the detail, or you may request that the report throws to a new page after printing a sub-total so that the next group of items starts on a fresh page. There are two levels of sub-totalling, so you may have a 'Sub-group on expression', for example you may break your sales area down into sub-areas.

The next window is used to enter the items that you want to see appear on the report, usually database fieldnames:

Contents
Heading
Width   0
Decimal places
Total this column

This window may be repeated until you have entered all the items you want to see on the report. At the 'Contents' you supply the name of the field, at the 'Heading' a caption for the field, then the width you wish to allocate the field on the page, and the number of decimal places you want. Finally you indicate whether the contents of the field should be totalled at the end of the report. The width of the field will automatically be set to the width specified in the database but you may change it. The report items are not, of course, restricted to database fields; they may be expressions involving combinations of fields, or the results of functions, and so forth. For example, you might want to see the contents of a field such as Value multiplied by a fixed exchange rate. Assuming an exchange rate of 3.275, the expression would be Value*3.275. Remember that if you specify totalling you should specify the width of a field wide enough to allow the program to print the total, which will probably contain more digits than any individual field.

When you have defined the report, the details will be written to a file with the report name you have specified plus the extension .FRM, for example SALES.FRM. If subsequently you want to modify the report details you can either issue the same CREATE REPORT command again or use the MODIFY REPORT command; the two are identical. With Clipper, the REPORT utility is similarly used to create or modify. Whichever you choose, you have to specify the filename of the .FRM file. The screens will appear exactly as before but they will contain all the details you entered previously. A report item is deleted by using the CTRL and U combination of keys. When you have completed the changes you select the SAVE menu option and the changed report details will be written back to their .FRM file.

The CREATE SCREEN command

Syntax: CREATE SCREEN filename
 MODIFY SCREEN filename

Available only in dBASE III PLUS, the CREATE SCREEN command is a full screen menu-driven screen painter similar in purpose to the dFORMAT program that accompanied earlier versions of dBASE III. The screen may be saved to a .SCR file and modified on a later occasion by means of the MODIFY SCREEN command. When you have set up the screen to your satisfaction, you can generate @ SAY and @ GET commands to be placed in an .FMT format file. The latter will have the same name as the .SCR file and may be activated by a SET FORMAT TO command and used by a READ command. The CREATE/ MODIFY SCREEN commands will also let you create or modify a database file.

The CREATE VIEW command

Syntax: CREATE VIEW filename [FROM ENVIRONMENT]
 MODIFY VIEW filename

CREATE VIEW is a dBASE III PLUS command used to create a new view file for use by the SET VIEW TO command. It is a full screen command that allows you to select database files, associated index files, work areas, relationships between database files, fields selected by the SET FIELDS command, and so forth, and store these details in a .VUE view file. By issuing the SET VIEW TO command and specifying the filename of the .VUE file, all the selected files will be opened and the relationships established. The entire working environment may thus be recreated on another occasion in one command:

```
set view to filename
```

The CREATE VIEW filename FROM ENVIRONMENT command will create a .VUE file containing details of the current working environment, i.e. the names of all open database files and associated indexes, selected work areas including relationships created by the SET RELATION TO command, open format files, and so forth.

The .VUE file may be modified with the MODIFY VIEW command, another full screen operation.

The DECLARE command

Syntax: DECLARE array name [numeric expression]

The DECLARE command is a Clipper only command that may be used to declare one or more arrays. The numeric expression, which has to be given in square brackets, indicates the number of elements in the array. Note that square brackets in a syntax line usually means that the clause is optional. In this case, however, they form part of the clause, for example:

```
declare costs[20], prices[20]
```

As you can see from the example, more than one array can be declared in the same DECLARE command. The square brackets are also used as a subscript to indicate which of the array elements is to be used when you access the array:

```
store costs[4] to curcost
store 5 to subscript
store prices[subscript] to curprice
```

The elements in an array do not have to be of the same type; they are given the type of the expressions assigned to them. Indeed, you may look upon an array as no more than a number of memory variables having the same name and distinguished by the subscript in square brackets. Note that the DECLARE command does not bring array elements into being; they do not exist until you create them with a STORE command. You can destroy the array and release its elements by assigning a value to it without specifying a subscript:

```
store 0 to costs
```

Array elements cannot be saved to .MEM files with the SAVE command. The LEN( ) function will return not the aggregate of the lengths of the array elements but the number of elements. The TYPE( ) function will return 'A' for an array.

The DELETE command

Syntax: DELETE [scope] [FOR/WHILE condition]

The DELETE command is used to remove records from the database file. It is, however, only the first step in the process since it does not itself physically delete records from the database: it simply marks them for future deletion. Physical deletion is carried out by the PACK command.

At the beginning of each record in the database is one character that is used by the DELETE command to set the deletion marker. The same character is used by the PACK and other commands to tell them whether the record has been marked for deletion. When such records are listed, they are indicated by an asterisk to the left of the first field. Records which have been marked for deletion may be retrieved by using the RECALL command, provided the PACK command has not yet been issued.

The scope clauses allow you to limit the DELETE command, for example by specifying the NEXT one or more records, or by using the RECORD clause to delete a specific record. The FOR/WHILE clauses allow you to impose conditions on the records to be processed in the course of the DELETE command. Used on its own the DELETE command will mark only the current record.

The SET DELETED ON command may be used to hide deleted records from the majority of dBASE commands. For example, commands such as FIND or COUNT will ignore the existence in the database file of records marked for deletion. The reverse is true if you issue the SET DELETED OFF command.

The DELETE FILE command

Syntax: DELETE FILE filename

The DELETE FILE command is used to remove database files, index files, or any other unwanted files from a diskette or directory. Note that you cannot delete a file which has not been closed, for example an attempt to delete a database file which is still in USE will result in an error message.

In the dBASE II specification the filename may be supplied without an extension, in which case a .DBF extension is assumed. In the dBASE III specification it is necessary to supply the full filename including the extension. In the latter, by the way, the correct command to use is ERASE; DELETE FILE has been maintained only to ensure consistency with dBASE II and will not be found in the documentation.

The DIR command

Syntax: DIR [filespec]

The DIR command provides a list of files in the current directory. It follows the same rules as the DOS DIR command except that used on its own it will display only .DBF files. In doing so, however, it does provide extra information, as the following example illustrates:

```
Database files      records    last update      size
NAMES.DBF               222     12/23/85        91629
MOTOR.DBF                 0     01/11/86          291
```

If used with a skeleton, it differs from the DOS DIR command in that it assumes the /W option:

```
NAMES.DBF            MOTOR.DBF
```

If you do want the DOS style vertical list of files, you should use the RUN command to execute the DOS DIR command. The DIR and RUN commands are not available in the dBASE II specification. The dBASE II equivalent to DIR is DISPLAY FILES.

The DISPLAY command

Syntax: DISPLAY [scope] [field list] [FOR/WHILE condition]
[OFF] [TO PRINT]

In describing the DISPLAY command, the opportunity is taken to give attention to the SCOPE and FOR/WHILE clauses, and dBASE operators such as .AND. or *. These are not explained elsewhere, since to do so in each command would simply duplicate what is covered here. The examples given below rely on familiarity with the structure of the database in USE. The structure given below supports these examples:

```
Structure for database : C:motor.dbf
Field  Field name  Type        Width   Dec
    1  MAKE        Character      10
    2  MODEL       Character       8
    3  TYPE        Character       8
    4  USER        Character      17
    5  VALUE       Numeric         8     2
** Total **                       52
```

The DISPLAY command is used to look at the contents of the current record of the database file in USE but the SCOPE of the command may be extended to other records.

Entering DISPLAY on its own will display the current record in full. Fields will appear in the sequence they were specified during the CREATE function, and each field will occupy its maximum number of positions, for example 17 for the name of the User.

Each record will be preceded by its record number unless the clause

OFF has been specified. Records that exceed the width of the screen will be folded so that any excess occupies the next line(s) down.

If the words TO PRINT are included in the command or the SET PRINT ON command has been issued previously the list will also appear on the printer. The TO PRINT clause is not available in dBASE II. The illustration below shows the results of the DISPLAY command on the MOTOR database file:

```
display next 3
Record   MAKE       MODEL    TYPE     USER              VALUE
      1  BMW        316      Saloon   Roberts, A G     7614.00
      2  BMW        320i     Saloon   MacKenzie,P      9370.00
      3  Mercedes   200TC    Estate   Smart,W R       11070.00
```

The example above also illustrates the use of the SCOPE clause which allows you to extend the command beyond the current record by specifying the number of records to be processed with the NEXT clause. If you want to DISPLAY all records from the current record to the end of the file, use the REST clause instead of NEXT:

```
display rest
```

Another useful way of employing the SCOPE clause is to specify ALL instead of NEXT or REST: this will display every record in the database, the equivalent of the LIST command but with the difference that the display will pause after every 15 records in the case of dBASE II, or 20 records in the case of dBASE III.

The final SCOPE clause is RECORD which allows you to specify a single record:

```
display record 115
```

This will do more than display the record; it will also move the current record pointer to record 115. Note that any DISPLAY operation which invokes the scope clause will move the current record pointer to the final record included in the specified SCOPE. The dBASE II specification does not support REST.

In addition to record number suppression and the SCOPE of the command, the DISPLAY command may be enhanced by adding one or both of the following:

- The fields to be listed
- Selection criteria

The fields to be listed

These are supplied in the sequence you want to see them appear (left to right). Fieldnames are separated by commas on the command line:

```
display next 3 make,model
Record    make          model
       1  BMW           316
       2  BMW           320i
       3  Mercedes      200TC
```

A field may be given as part of an expression, for example with a function such as SUBSTR or TRIM. Fields may be combined or character fields may be joined to character strings with the + operator. In the following example the trailing spaces are removed from the Make, but a character string consisting of a single space enclosed in quote marks is added to separate the Make from the Model:

```
display next 3 trim(make)+' '+model
Record    trim(make)+' '+model
       1  BMW 316
       2  BMW 320i
       3  Mercedes 200TC
```

You may apply constants to produce expressions such as Value*.35, i.e. Value times .35, to obtain a 35% figure of the value of each vehicle. The standard dBASE arithmetical operators are:

 * multiplication
 / division
 + addition
 − subtraction
 ** exponentiation (not dBASE II)

Round brackets, i.e ( ), are used to group operations in complex expessions. This apart, the sequence in which the operators are applied is left to right.

The fields being displayed may reside in more that one dBASE database file. In the dBASE II specification two files may be open at the same time. Provided you used the SELECT PRIMARY/SECON-DARY commands correctly, you could simply use the fieldnames from the two database files. If the same fieldname occurred in both databases, you would distinguish them by prefixing the fieldname with a p. or s. to indicate primary or secondary respectively.

In the dBASE III specification, where several databases may be open at the same time, it is necessary to prefix the fieldname with the work area identifier or ALIAS. The work area identifiers start at the letter a and continue to b, c, d, e, f and so on for each subsequent work area. A field is tied to a work area by prefixing the fieldname with the work area identifier and an arrow made up of a dash and a 'greater than' sign, for example:

display b−>make,b−>model

As in dBASE II, the work areas must previously have been specified with the SELECT command. As an alternative to the work area indentifiers, it is possible to use meaningful aliases in their place. This is done by specifying an ALIAS at the time the database file is opened, and then subsequently simply using the ALIAS in place of the work area identifier:

```
use motor alias anything
display anything->make,anything->model
```

If you do not specify an ALIAS in the USE command, the ALIAS is set equal to the filename which means that you may use the filename itself as the ALIAS:

```
use motor
display motor->make,motor->model
```

Bear in mind that the DISPLAY command operates on the current record and does not necessarily take care of moving on to the next record in each of the database files represented by fieldnames in a DISPLAY command. The clauses which extend its activities to additional records, such as the SCOPE clause, typically only move the operation on in the currently SELECTED database file (see SELECT command). A method of accomplishing simultaneous movement in all the required database files is to use the SET RELATION TO command.

Note, too, that in Clipper you must specify the fieldname(s) to be displayed: the DISPLAY command on its own is invalid. Nor does Clipper display the fieldnames as headings at the beginning of the display as in the examples above.

The selection criteria

These allow you to specify which records you want to include in your list. Records not meeting the specified conditions will be ignored. For example, to display only BMWs you would enter the following:

```
display next 3 for make = 'BMW'
Record   MAKE      MODEL    TYPE     USER                VALUE
      1  BMW       316      Saloon   Roberts, A G        7614.00
      2  BMW       320i     Saloon   MacKenzie,P         9370.00
```

Note that you have to provide the correct combination of upper and lower-case. For example, 'bmw' will not succeed in listing any records. A way around this is to use the upper-case function (! in the dBASE II specification, UPPER in the dBASE III specification) which will convert lower-case characters to upper-case. Thus the following would display records containing Saloon, saloon, or SALOON as the Type of vehicle:

```
display for upper(type) = 'SALOON'
```

Any character constant is enclosed in quote marks. If the field being tested had been a numeric one, for example DISPLAY FOR VALUE > 10000, the constant would simply be shown as a numeric value.

The selection criteria may be quite complex and cover more than one field:

```
display for make = 'BMW' .and. value > 10000
```

Record	MAKE	MODEL	TYPE	USER	VALUE
7	BMW	735i	Saloon	Richards,P G	19750.00
9	BMW	323i	Saloon	Andrews,J H	10320.00

The example above illustrates the use of two comparison operators, equal to and greater than. The full set of comparison operators are:

=	: equal
# or <>	: not equal
<	: less than
>	: greater than
<=	: less than or equal
>=	: greater than or equal
$	: equal or contained in, for example 'ar'$User will select Smart, W R and Richards, P G

A selection based on two or more conditions is specified using logical operators:

```
.and.   : make = 'BMW' .and. type = 'Saloon'
.or.    : make = 'BMW' .or. make = 'Mercedes'
.not.   : .not. type = 'Estate'
```

The .NOT. operator is used to apply an exclusion. To display all vehicles other than BMWs over 20000 in value, you would enter:

```
display for .not. (make='BMW' .and. value > 20000)
```

The examples above have all been based on the FOR clause where all records are examined to see whether they meet the selection criteria. Another very similar clause, the WHILE clause, will perform the same function but can be more economical in terms of time. It assumes that the starting record (which need not be the first record on the file) meets the condition and it will stop dBASE reading any further once the condition is no longer being met:

```
go 1
display while make = 'BMW'
Record   MAKE      MODEL    TYPE     USER              VALUE
     1   BMW       316      Saloon   Roberts, A G    7614.00
     2   BMW       320i     Saloon   MacKenzie,P     9370.00
```

In dBASE III PLUS you may use the FOR clause as a sub-selection to the WHILE clause within the same command:

```
go 1
display while make = 'BMW'for value>8000
Record   MAKE      MODEL    TYPE     USER              VALUE
     2   BMW       320i     Saloon   MacKenzie,P     9370.00
```

The DISPLAY FILES command

Syntax: DISPLAY FILES [LIKE skeleton] [ON drive]

The DISPLAY FILES command is used to obtain a directory listing. Used on its own, it provides a list of database files in the current directory, such as the following dBASE II example:

```
DATABASE FILES    RCDS    LAST UPDATE
MOTOR     DBF     00001   11/26/86
SHOPPING DBF      00057   08/16/86
FILE      DBF     00006   11/26/86
BANKS     DBF     00015   06/21/86
SERNO     DBF     00027   07/30/86
```

In dBASE III the equivalent command is DIR, but DISPLAY FILES is nevertheless included to provide compatibility with dBASE II. Clipper relies only on DIR; it does not recognise DISPLAY FILES.

Like DIR, the DISPLAY FILES command may specify a skeleton but unlike DIR the keyword LIKE has to be used:

```
display files like *.prg
SHOPPING.PRG        STAFF   .PRG      BANKS   .PRG      DEPT    .PRG
STAFF   .PRG        DEPT    .PRG      TAPES2  .PRG      FRED    .PRG
INPUT   .PRG        MARIO   .PRG      MDPTAPES.PRG
```

Also like DIR, the DISPLAY FILES command may specify a drive but the keyword ON has to be used:

```
display files like *.prg on b:
```

The LIST FILES command is an alternative to the DISPLAY FILES command, but does not pause during the display.

The DISPLAY HISTORY command

Syntax: DISPLAY HISTORY [LAST numeric expression]
[TO PRINT]

This dBASE III PLUS command will display the most recent interactive commands that have been issued up to a maximum of 20 command lines, for example:

```
. display history
use names
set index to names
find LAND
disp name,commission
list for area="SW" .and. commission>15 .and. sales>10000
replace commission with commission*1.05 for area="SW" .and. sales>10000
display history
```

The HISTORY feature is essentially a device for use during interactive processing. It allows you to change and repeat a previous command, for example one that might have been entered incorrectly. The up arrow key will display previous commands one by one and it will do so at the dot prompt. When the required command appears, you can use the normal editing rules to change the command, and the Return key to execute it. The down arrow key may be used to display the commands one by one in reverse sequence.

You may change the number of lines that will be stored as history with the SET HISTORY TO command. If you want to include command lines executed by a DO command, i.e. those contained in a .PRG file, you may do so with the SET DOHISTORY ON command. You can also turn off the HISTORY feature with the SET HISTORY OFF command.

The DISPLAY HISTORY command will pause during the display if the screen has been filled. The number of lines being displayed may be limited to the number specified by the LAST keyword. You may also indicate that the display is to be printed.

The DISPLAY MEMORY command

Syntax: DISPLAY MEMORY [TO PRINT]

The DISPLAY MEMORY command is used to look at the contents of active memory variables. It displays the names, types and contents of memory variables.

You may also add the TO PRINT clause to send the details to the printer. This is not available in the dBASE II specification but the same effect may be obtained by using the SET PRINT ON command before issuing the DISPLAY MEMORY command. Clipper does not support the DISPLAY MEMORY command but the same function is available in the separate debugger utility that accompanies the compiler.

The DISPLAY STATUS command

Syntax: DISPLAY STATUS [TO PRINT]

The DISPLAY STATUS command is used to find out which database files and indexes are currently in USE, the current settings of the on/off kind of SET commands, and so on. One of the most useful features of this command is the fact that it displays the keys of all active index files, as in the following dBASE III example:

```
. display status
Currently selected database:
Select area -  1, Database in use: C:motor.dbf
    Index file: C:cars.ndx  key - make+model
    Index file: C:cost.ndx  key - value
```

In the dBASE III specification you may add the TO PRINT clause to send the details to the printer. In the dBASE II specification the same effect may be obtained by using the SET PRINT ON command before issuing the DISPLAY STATUS command. Clipper does not support the DISPLAY STATUS command but the same function is available in the separate debugger utility that accompanies the compiler.

If you are working at the screen, the DISPLAY STATUS command is preferable to the near-identical LIST STATUS command since it pauses in the course of producing the listing.

The DISPLAY STRUCTURE command

Syntax: DISPLAY STRUCTURE [TO PRINT]

The DISPLAY STRUCTURE command, as its name implies shows the structure of the database file currently in USE, for example:

```
Structure for database : C:motor.dbf
Number of data records :      178
Date of last update    : 12/12/86
Field  Field name  Type        Width    Dec
    1  MAKE        Character      10
    2  MODEL       Character       8
    3  USER        Character      17
    4  VALUE       Numeric         9      2
    5  YEAR        Numeric         2
    6  NOTES       Memo           10
    7  MILES       Numeric         5
    8  LASTDATE    Date            8
** Total **                      70
```

It also shows the number of records and the date the database file was last changed.

In the dBASE III specification you may add the TO PRINT clause to send the details to the printer. In the dBASE II specification the same effect may be obtained by using the SET PRINT ON command before issuing the DISPLAY STRUCTURE command. Clipper does not support the DISPLAY STRUCTURE command. DISPLAY STRUC-TURE will pause after every 15 (dBASE II) or 16 (dBASE III) fields.

The DO command

Syntax: DO filename/procedure name [WITH parameter list]

The DO command executes a separate program module in a .PRG file or a procedure in a procedure file. The WITH clause is the counterpart of the PARAMETERS command in the called procedure or program, and the WITH parameter list in the DO command should therefore match the parameter list in the PARAMETERS command. Let us look at an example:

```
do cubecalc with 3,5,4,cube
.
.
.
procedure cubecalc
parameters w,x,y,z
z = w*x*y
return
```

In the example above, the local variables W,X,Y and Z are assigned to receive the values passed by the calling program. When the RETURN command is executed, the values contained in W,X,Y and Z are passed back so that when control returns to the calling module, the variable CUBE will contain the value that the variable Z had in the called procedure.

Parameters can be passed by value or by reference. If the parameter being passed is an expression, the value of the expression is evaluated and passed to be placed in a local variable. If the parameter is the name of a memory variable it is passed by reference, i.e. the value is used from the variable in the calling program. Such a variable may be changed by the called module, even though it is using the locally assigned name, and the change will be effective in the calling program. The following illustrates this point:

```
clear all
store 2 to height,width,length
store 0 to cube
do cubecalc with height,length,width,cube
disp memo
return


procedure cubecalc
para w,x,y,z
z = w*x*y
store 9 to w
disp memo
return
```

The first memory display, i.e. that contained in the called procedure, looks like this:

```
HEIGHT       priv  (hidden)  N          9
WIDTH        priv  (hidden)  N          2
LENGTH       priv  (hidden)  N          2
CUBE         priv  (hidden)  N          8
W            priv  a   HEIGHT
X            priv  a   LENGTH
Y            priv  a   WIDTH
Z            priv  a   CUBE
```

As you can see, the cube was correctly calculated using a height of 2, and the contents of the variable HEIGHT in the calling program were then changed to another value. The memory display in the calling program confirms the change:

```
HEIGHT       priv  N          9
WIDTH        priv  N          2
LENGTH       priv  N          2
CUBE         priv  N          8
```

In the dBASE II specification there are no procedures, nor can you use the WITH clause since there is no parameter passing.

The DO CASE command

Syntax: DO CASE
        CASE condition
          commands
        [CASE condition
          commands]
        [OTHERWISE
          commands]
      ENDCASE

The DO CASE command enables you to select a single course of action from a number of alternatives. The command is frequently used in processing menus where the user is able to select one menu option at a time, for example:

```
do while .t.
  clear
  store ' ' to option
  a 1,0 say 'FLEET MANAGEMENT'
  a 5,0 say '1. Enter information'
  a 6,0 say '2. Change existing information'
  a 7,0 say '3. Look up an item of information'
  a 8,0 say '4. Produce a printed report'
  a 9,0 say 'X. Exit'
  do while .not. option$'1234X'
    a 13,0 say 'Enter your choice ' get option picture '!'
    read
  enddo
  do case
    case option = 'X'
      clear
      quit
    case option = '1'
      do cars1
    case option = '2'
      do cars2
    case option = '3'
      do cars3
    case option = '4'
      do cars4
  endcase
enddo
```

When a condition in a CASE clause is evaluated as True, all subsequent commands up to the next CASE, OTHERWISE or ENDCASE line are executed. Control then skips to the command following the ENDCASE line. If the condition is evaluated as False, control moves on to the next CASE, OTHERWISE or ENDCASE line. The OTHERWISE clause will be evaluated as True if *all* the CASE conditions are evaluated as False. The ENDCASE line marks the end of the DO CASE command.

The DO WHILE command

Syntax: DO WHILE condition
           commands
     ENDDO

The DO WHILE command enables you to perform a DO loop. This means that the commands between the DO WHILE line and the ENDDO line will be executed repeatedly while the condition specified in the command evaluates as True. If the condition is evaluated as False, execution will pass immediately to the command following the ENDDO line:

```
store " " to option
do while .not. option$'1234X'
  a 13,0 say 'Enter your choice ' get option picture '!'
  read
enddo
```

If the EXIT command is encountered within the DO loop, it will take execution control out of the DO loop and pass it to the command following the ENDDO. Similarly, the LOOP command will pass control back to the beginning of the DO loop. Remember to be careful of using macros in the DO WHILE condition in dBASE III and dBASE III PLUS as explained in Chapter 2, page 20.

The EDIT command

dBASE II syntax:
    EDIT [record number]
dBASE III syntax:
    EDIT [scope] [FIELDS field list] [FOR/WHILE condition]

The EDIT command is a full screen command which is essentially interactive although it is possible to use it in a program provided you do not mind taking the risk of losing control, for example through its ability to move on to other records under user control rather than under program control.

In the dBASE II specification EDIT expects the record number, which may be presented as a number or as an expression. If the record number is not supplied, it will ask for it. The record number, by the way, is supplied without the RECORD keyword: the latter is not recognised in the dBASE II specification.

In the dBASE III specification, EDIT on its own will present the current record. You may ask for a specific record by quoting the record number as in dBASE II, with or without the RECORD keyword. You may also specify the name of a memory variable containing the record number.

The standard dBASE control keys are used during the operation of the EDIT command, for example CTRL and C or PgDn to move on a record or CTRL and R or PgUp to move back a record, CTRL and X or down arrow to move on a field or CTRL and E or up arrow to move back field. You leave the EDIT command by pressing CTRL and W or CTRL and End to save the changes made to the current record, or CTRL and Q or the Escape key to leave without saving the changes.

A Memo field is edited by placing the cursor on the field and then pressing the CTRL and PgDn key. You return from the word processing environment by using the CTRL and PgUp keys. Memo fields are not available in the dBASE II specification. In Clipper a special MEMO-EDIT function is available to edit Memo fields.

The EDIT command has no means of validating the details that are entered other than to check for format, i.e. it will ensure that character data is not entered in a numeric field but will not concern itself with the accuracy or otherwise of the numeric information. Do take care, therefore, if you are preparing an application for the use of others never to let them use the EDIT command. A simple program sequence using the @ GET command, which has PICTURE validation and in the dBASE III specification includes a useful RANGE clause, is much safer. The use of a program rather than the EDIT command also enables you to check user-entered items against lists of valid codes coded as part of your program or held in other database files. The EDIT command is not supported by the Clipper compiler. In dBASE III PLUS, the EDIT command is identical to the CHANGE command.

The EJECT Command

Syntax: EJECT

This command is directed at the printer and causes it to move the paper up to the next start of page (or top of form).

In dBASE II, the EJECT command has no effect unless the SET PRINT ON or SET FORMAT TO PRINT commands have previously been issued. In dBASE III this is no longer true.

The EJECT command will reset the printer coordinates to 0,0 for @ SAY or @ GET commands, and for the PROW( ) and PCOL( ) functions. The EJECT command is, of course, essential in any report where a new page is required after a sub-total has been printed or on a change of category, for example when the make of car changes from BMW to Mercedes.

EJECT can be particularly useful at the end of a print program to ensure that the final page of a report or listing is not left halfway up in the printer. Some programmers even follow the practice of issuing a double EJECT at the end of a printed report to leave the paper at a point where the sheet containing the last page of the report can be torn off without manually advancing the paper. In the case of page printers such as the HP Laserjet, the EJECT command is essential at the end of the print operation since the printer does not begin its print cycle until it knows that there are no more lines for the page.

The ERASE command

Syntax: ERASE
        ERASE filename

The ERASE command, like the CLEAR command, suffers from two very different interpretations in the dBASE II and dBASE III specifications. In the former it performs the job of the dBASE III CLEAR command, i.e. all it does is clear the screen. Not quite all, since it also clears pending @ GETs, but it nevertheless follows the same rules as the dBASE III CLEAR command.

In the dBASE III specification, the ERASE command is used to delete a file from the disk directory. You cannot delete a file which has not been closed, for example an attempt to delete a database file which is still in USE will result in an error message. Also, it is necessary to supply the full filename including the extension.

The EXIT command

Syntax: EXIT

The EXIT command is not available in the dBASE II specification. The purpose of this command is to escape from a DO loop by transferring control to the instruction immediately following the ENDDO command. It has a similar application to the LOOP command in that both avoid the execution of subsequent commands within the DO loop, except that the LOOP command transfers control to the beginning of the DO loop, i.e. it repeats the loop, while EXIT leaves the loop.

Take care to use this command correctly: it will always refer to the nearest ENDDO command which may not be the one you had in mind, particularly if you are using nested loops, i.e. loops within loops.

The FIND command

Syntax: FIND string/number

The FIND command operates on the main index currently in use. It searches the index file for a key that matches the string or number specified in the FIND command. When it has found a matching key, it will use the record number contained in that index entry to establish the corresponding record as the current record. The whole process takes place within a second or two. Following the FIND command, the contents of such a record may be accessed by any of the commands which operate on the current record, for example STORE, REPLACE, @ SAY, and so on.

It is, however, necessary to test that the match was successful. In the dBASE II specification this is done by testing the current record number using the # function: if this function returns a current record number of zero, you know that there was no match. In the dBASE III specification the same test is performed by using the EOF( ) or end of file function: if this function returns an answer of True, there has been no match. As an alternative you could use the FOUND( ) function which returns a logical True if there has been a match.

The string specified in the FIND command has to correspond to the beginning of the key but may be shorter than the key. Case differences are observed, i.e. an upper-case string will not match on a key which is held in lower-case. A useful method of getting around this restriction is to apply the upper-case function to the key field(s) when creating the index. If you then consistently use an upper-case string in all FIND commands, the case differences will not matter. Note that a string used in the FIND command does not require delimiters such as quotes or square brackets unless the string contains embedded spaces. You may, for example, have created an index as follows:

```
index on upper(customer)+custcode to customer
```

If the Customer field is 8 characters long, there will be trailing spaces after a name like JONES, so that the FIND command could look like this:

```
. find JONES    5041
no find
. find "JONES    5041"
. display customer
0047   Jones
```

As you can see, the quotes delimiter has been used to tell the FIND command to include the second string. The use of a delimiter may also be necessary if the STR function has been used in setting up an index (see page 19 in Chapter 2)

We have so far been discussing character string keys, but you may have used a numeric key in setting up an index. In this case you would specify the number to be found by the FIND command. The complete number has to be given but there is no need to supply leading zeros since dBASE will convert the number you supply to match the length of the key in the index entry.

Macro substitution is very important in the FIND command as a means of using memory variables:

```
. store "JONES" to keyval
. find &keyval
```

If you do not know what key you want to FIND until you have obtained the key from the user by means of an @...GET or ACCEPT command, you will have to use macro substitution to tell dBASE to look for the key in the specified memory variable. In dBASE III the alternative is to use the SEEK command which operates on a memory variable instead of directly on the string or number.

The FOR/NEXT command

Syntax: FOR memory variable = numeric expression TO numeric
          expression [STEP numeric expression]
       command(s)
       NEXT

FOR/NEXT is a Clipper only command that will be familiar to those
who have used BASIC as a means of executing a loop a fixed number of
times, at the same time incrementing (or decrementing) the variable that
controls the loop. The example below illustrates its use:

```
for i = 11 to 70
   a 1,i  say "*"
   a 19,i say "*"
next
```

The loop will be executed once for every value of the variable 'i' from 11
to 70. The variable is incremented by one unless you use the optional
STEP clause to specify a different increment, for example:

```
for i = 1 to 3 step .2
   ? rate*i
next
```

The NEXT line represents the end of the loop. The value in the variable
may be decremented by specifying the higher value first:

```
for i = 10 to 1
   a i,0 say "+"
next
```

The numeric expression in the STEP clause may be positive or negative.

The FUNCTION command

Syntax: FUNCTION name

       .

       .

       .

       RETURN value

FUNCTION is a Clipper only command that is used to create your
own functions. The following is an example of such as a function:

```
FUNCTION MAX
*
* Syntax : MAX(a,b)
          where :
                    a : numeric expression 1
                    b : numeric expression 2
* Returns : The greater of two numbers
*
PARAMETERS num1, num2
RETURN IF(num1 > num2, num1, num2)
```

A user defined function is invoked from within a program in exactly the same way as you would execute a standard dBASE function, for example:

```
store max(cost1,cost2) to highcost
```

The RETURN command must include an expression that is returned to the command line using the function. A more detailed account of the FUNCTION command is given at the end of Chapter 6.

The GO/GOTO command

Syntax: GO/GOTO numeric expression
        GO/GOTO BOTTOM
        GO/GOTO TOP

The GO or GOTO command positions you at a certain record which then becomes the current record. In both dBASE II and dBASE III specifications, the word GO or GOTO is optional since the record number on its own acts as an alternative:

```
. ? recno()
        5
. 26
. ? recno()
        26
```

In the Clipper compiler the word GO or GOTO must be included. The record number may be specified as a value, as in the example above, or it may be contained in a memory variable:

```
. store 39 to recpoint
. go recpoint
. ? recno()
        39
```

An alternative to using the record number is to specify TOP or

BOTTOM which refer respectively to the first or last record on the database. If no index is in use, this will be in relation to the physical sequence of the database file. Otherwise the first and last record will reflect the sequence of records in the index that controls the sequence of the database.

In a dBASE program, the GO command plus record number is less likely to be used than the FIND/SEEK command. The latter operates intelligently with a meaningful index, for example one based on surnames, while this form of the GO command is limited to the physical position of a record, an item of knowledge which is of complete indifference to the user. The GO TOP or GO BOTTOM commands are more useful because they position you at a known starting point.

The IF command

Syntax: IF condition
      commands
   [ELSE
      commands]
   ENDIF

The IF command executes the commands between the IF line and its paired ENDIF if the condition evaluates as True, otherwise control passes to the command following the paired ENDIF. The ELSE clause may be introduced to provide the means of executing one set of commands within the IF/ENDIF pair if the condition is True, and another – those following the ELSE – if it is False. You may nest IF/ENDIF pairs within one another:

```
if next = "+"
  if .not. eof()
    skip
    store 1 to endx
  else
    store 0 to endx
  endif     [if EOF endx will be 0]
else
  if .not. bof()
    skip -1
    store 1 to endx
  else
    store 0 to endx
  endif     [if BOF endx will be 0]
endif
```

Note again the use of indentation to show up the IF/ENDIF pairs, and the use of comments.

The INDEX command

Syntax: INDEX ON expression TO filename [UNIQUE]

The INDEX command creates a separate index file using the filename specified in the command together with the filename extension .NDX (dBASE II, dBASE III, and FoxBASE) or .NTX (Clipper).

The purpose of the index file is twofold. It provides a means of sequencing the database information without actually disturbing the database itself, and it enables you to find a particular record within seconds. An index file holds an entry for every record in the database, each entry containing a key and the record number of the record to which the key contents refer.

The key is made up of fields or combinations of fields from the database file currently in USE, as dictated by the expression defined in the ON clause. The keys are usually held in ascending sequence although numeric keys may be held in descending sequence. The full freedom of dBASE expressions is allowed within the INDEX command so that you may index a file on the results of a calculation or a combination of functions, for example:

```
index on substr(dtoc(startdate),7,2) to startyr
```

It is possible to gauge the size of an index file, although the size will change as extra records are added at various places in the indexing sequence. As an example let us look at the index files of dBASE II and dBASE III. Both use a B+ tree structure for their indexes, and the calculation looks like this:

1. Number of entries per index record:
   dBASE II :   509 divided by (key length + 4)
   dBASE III : 509 divided by (key length + 8)

2. Number of index records:
   Number of records in the database divided by number of entries per index record.

3. Index file size:
   Smallest : Number of index records times 512 bytes.
   Largest :   Number of index records times 2 times 512 bytes

While the dBASE specification allows several index files to be open at the same time so that they may all be updated by the addition of new database records and so forth, the INDEX command will reset the status to that of just the index file specified in the command. After executing the INDEX command, you will therefore have to use the SET INDEX TO command if you want to reintroduce the other index files. Also remember that the SET INDEX TO command resets all the indexes, so you have to include the names of all the index files you require, including the one you have just indexed. And where several index files are open at the same time, only the first will dictate the sequence of the database. In dBASE III PLUS the SET ORDER TO command may be used to change the controlling index without having to reissue the SET INDEX TO command.

The UNIQUE clause was introduced by dBASE III PLUS, although in dBASE III versions earlier than dBASE III PLUS it has an equivalent in the SET UNIQUE ON command. UNIQUE means that you do not want the indexing operation to include duplicate keys.

The index files of the various implementations of the dBASE language are not compatible with one another. A dBASE II index file cannot be used with dBASE III or FoxBASE, nor are dBASE III and Clipper index files interchangeable. These differences are not too significant, however, since you simply use the INDEX command to recreate your indexes when you change from one to another. Thus if you were moving from dBASE II to FoxBASE you would use the FoxBASE INDEX command to set up FoxBASE indexes. And if you were moving to dBASE III you would find that the dCONVERT program creates a short program file for each index which contains the INDEX command and the appropriate key. You are expected to execute the program yourself after you have loaded dBASE III. A good programming habit in this context consists of including in your programs a test for the index file using the FILE( ) function, and the INDEX command to create the index if the FILE( ) test fails.

The INPUT command

Syntax: INPUT ['prompt'] TO variable

The INPUT command may be used as an alternative to the @ GET command to ask the user for information from the keyboard (see also the ACCEPT command). The prompt is optional but is valuable in explaining to the user what is being asked, for example:

```
input "Please enter Cost of Vehicle " to costx
```

Note the extra space at the end of the prompt. If this is not supplied, the user's response will begin immediately after the prompt, so that the screen could look like this:

```
Please enter Cost of Vehicle12000
```

In the dBASE II specification, a colon appears to the right of the prompt. The INPUT command will accept any valid dBASE expression: the latter will determine the type of the variable that receives the data. Thus, if the user enters a string with quote marks before and after, the data will be interpreted as character data so that the variable receiving the data will become a character variable. If the user response is 56.87, the resulting variable will be numeric, and so on. You do not need to initialise a variable in order to use it in the INPUT command: it will be created if it does not already exist.

Note that the INPUT command is self-contained: it does not have to be followed by a READ command as does the @ GET command. With INPUT, as soon as the Return key is pressed the user's entry is passed to the program. The drawback of this command is that you cannot format the entry field in the way that the @ GET command does with the PICTURE clause.

An important point to consider is that it is possible to generate a syntax error (in either the dBASE II or dBASE III specification) if the user simply presses the Return key without entering any data. In all cases this will lead to confusion for the user of the program, and loss of control over the application for the developer. Neither is desirable or even acceptable, which places a very large question mark over the wisdom of using the INPUT command at all when it comes to writing programs.

The INSERT command

Syntax: INSERT [BLANK] [BEFORE]

INSERT is essentially an interactive command, but even when you are working interactively it is usually preferable to use the APPEND command instead and rely on an index to maintain the required file sequence.

The INSERT command operates in relation to the current record, i.e. you are inserting a new record either before (if you include the BEFORE keyword), or following the current record. The BLANK keyword allows you to insert a record that has no data, the expectation being that you will subsequently fill the record by using a command such as REPLACE or EDIT.

The INSERT command causes the records in a database file to be moved along physically. As a consequence, it suffers from the drawbacks of potentially slow execution (particularly during an insertion at an early point in a very large file) as well as the risk of a corrupted file should the operation be interrupted by loss of power or other breakdown. In addition, you have to ensure that all your indexes for the database in question are updated to reflect the physical changes of record number.

Once the command has been issued, it behaves much as the EDIT command does, i.e. full screen cursor controls allow you to move from field to field and in the dBASE III specification you may access Memo fields with the CTRL and PgDn keys. In the dBASE II specification, you may insert only one record per INSERT command. In dBASE III you may keep adding extra records, all of which will be inserted at the same point in the database file. You leave the INSERT command by pressing CTRL and W or CTRL and End to save the currently entered details, or CTRL and Q or the Escape key to leave without saving the changes. The INSERT command is not supported by the Clipper compiler.

The JOIN command

dBASE II syntax:
    JOIN TO filename FOR condition
    FIELDS field list]
dBASE III syntax:
    JOIN WITH alias TO filename FOR condition
    [FIELDS field list]

The JOIN command combines the structure and contents of two separate databases. The resulting database is specified with the TO clause while the FOR clause specifies the condition under which records are to be combined, usually a matter of testing whether a field from one database file is equal to a field from the second database file. For example, you might JOIN a name and address database with an employee database to obtain a database containing both sets of details, and you would match on employee name:

```
. use empnames
. join with staff to staff2 for surname = b->empname ;
     fields empname,dept,addr1,addr2,addr3,telno
```

What happens in the course of executing the JOIN command is that dBASE starts with the first record on the currently selected or active database and reads through the whole of the second database, comparing the field(s) specified in the FOR condition of the command. Those in the current record of the active database are compared with the specified field(s) in each record of the second database. When it finds a match, it writes the requested fields (as specified by the FIELDS clause) from both records to the database specified by the TO clause. The structure of the latter is determined by the fields specified in the JOIN command. If you do not specify the FIELDS clause, all the fields from both databases will be included.

When dBASE has read through to the end of the second database file, it moves on to the second record on the active file and reads through the second file again, looking for a match on the fields specified in the FOR clause. This sequence is repeated until every record on the active database file has been read, i.e. the second database file is read as many times as there are records on the active database file.

The condition specified in the JOIN command need not be restricted to the matching fields. You could extend it to include other criteria, for example to include only those in the Sales department by adding an AND clause to the command, as in the following example:

```
. use empnames
. join with staff to staff2 ;
     for surname = b->empname .and. b->dept = "SALES" ;
     fields empname,dept,addr1,addr2,addr3,telno
```

The potential number of records that could be created by the JOIN command is equal to the total number of records on the active database multiplied by the total number of records on the second database. Also, as has already been mentioned, if you do not specify a list of fields, the structure of the specified database will contain all the fields from the active database plus all the fields from the second database.

The main difference between the two syntaxes given above is that the dBASE II specification has only two work areas and thus two database files that may be joined, whereas the dBASE III specification allows several. In the latter case, therefore, it is necessary to introduce the WITH clause to select one of the several possible work areas.

The KEYBOARD command

Syntax: KEYBOARD character expression

KEYBOARD is a Clipper only command that may be used to insert characters into the keyboard buffer. This method is used to apply run time program control to the execution of other sections of the program. You could, for example, insert an 'X' followed by the value of the Return key into the keyboard buffer to force selection of the Exit menu option:

```
keyboard "X" + chr(13)
```

The KEYBOARD command may also be used to achieve the same effect as the CLEAR TYPEAHEAD command of dBASE III PLUS by supplying a null string:

```
keyboard ""
```

The LABEL command

Syntax: LABEL FORM filename [scope] [FOR/WHILE condition]
[TO PRINT] [TO FILE filename] [SAMPLE]

The LABEL command (available only in the dBASE III specification) is intended to help you to produce name and address labels from a dBASE database file. In practice, it can be used to do more than that, but let us begin by looking at its most basic use.

As a prerequisite it is necessary to have created an .LBL file which contains the definition of the labels to be produced by the LABEL command. Typically this presents a name on line 1 and an address on lines 2 onwards. The .LBL file is created either by the CREATE LABEL or MODIFY LABEL commands of dBASE III, or the LABEL utility of Clipper.

The LABEL command will interpret the definition specified in the filename of the FORM clause and produce labels according to instructions contained in the definition and using database records according to the scope and FOR/WHILE conditions. The SCOPE clause allows you to limit the command, for example by specifying the number of records (starting at the current record) to be processed with the NEXT clause.

If the words TO PRINT are included in the command or the SET PRINT ON command has been issued previously, the details will also appear on the printer. Similarly, the details may be written as print lines to a text file by using the TO FILE clause.

When you use label stationery you do, of course, have to align it correctly so that, for example, the first label does not start printing near the foot of a label or too far over to the right. To help you align the stationery according to the specifications you entered during the CREATE LABEL procedure, line-up labels will be printed if you include the clause SAMPLE in your command:

```
label form users sample to print

******************************          ******************************
******************************          ******************************
******************************          ******************************
******************************          ******************************
******************************          ******************************
******************************          ******************************

Do you want more samples?  (Y/N)
```

Having considered the LABEL command for names and addresses, it should be clear that this method can be a very effective way of presenting any information that you want to display in tabular format:

```
Ship      DANNIELLE           Ship      DESDEMONA
Club      UK P&I              Club      LONDON
Tonnage   95000               Tonnage   33500
Built     1956                Built     1972
```

Where sequence is important, however, you should bear in mind that the sequence in which records are displayed will be left, right, left, right, rather than a whole column on the left followed by a column on the right as you would find in a telephone directory.

The LIST command

Syntax: LIST [scope] [field list] [FOR/WHILE condition]
[OFF] [TO PRINT]

The LIST command is nearly identical to the DISPLAY command, the only differences being as follows:

1. LIST does not pause periodically: it continues to list records until the end of the database or the end of the SCOPE clause or WHILE clause has been reached.
2. If a SCOPE clause or the FOR/WHILE clause is not specified for the DISPLAY command, it will only display the current record. In the same circumstances, the LIST command will display all records.

The LIST FILES command

Syntax: LIST FILES [LIKE skeleton] [ON drive]

The LIST FILES command is identical to DISPLAY FILES and is used to obtain a directory listing. Used on its own, it provides a list of database files in the current directory, such as the following dBASE II example:

```
DATABASE FILES    RCDS    LAST UPDATE
MOTOR      DBF    00001   11/26/86
SHOPPING DBF      00057   08/16/86
FILE       DBF    00006   11/26/86
BANKS      DBF    00015   06/21/86
SERNO      DBF    00027   07/30/86
```

In the dBASE III specification, the equivalent command is DIR but LIST FILES is nevertheless included to provide compatibility with the dBASE II specification. Clipper relies only on DIR: it does not recognise LIST FILES.

As with DIR, the LIST FILES command may specify a skeleton, but unlike DIR the keyword LIKE has to be used:

```
list files like *.prg
```

```
SHOPPING.PRG       STAFF    .PRG     BANKS   .PRG      DEPT    .PRG
STAFF    .PRG       DEPT     .PRG     TAPES2  .PRG      FRED    .PRG
INPUT    .PRG       MARIO    .PRG     MDPTAPES.PRG
```

Also like DIR, the LIST FILES command may specify a drive, but the keyword ON has to be used:

```
list files like *.prg on b:
```

The LIST HISTORY command

Syntax: LIST HISTORY [LAST numeric expression] [TO PRINT]

This dBASE III PLUS command will display the most recent interactive commands that have been issued up to a maximum of 20 command lines, for example:

```
. list history
use names
set index to names
find LAND
disp name,commission
list for area="SW" .and. commission>15 .and. sales>10000
replace commission with commission*1.05 for area="SW" .and. sales>10000
list history
```

The HISTORY feature is essentially a device for use during interactive processing. It allows you to change and repeat a previous command, for example one that might have been entered incorrectly. The up arrow key will display previous commands one by one and it will do so at the dot prompt. When the required command appears, you can use the normal editing rules to change the command, and the Return key to execute it. The down arrow key may be used to display the commands one by one in reverse sequence.

You may change the number of lines that will be stored as history with the SET HISTORY TO command. If you want to include command lines executed by a DO command, i.e. those contained in a .PRG file, you may do so with the SET DOHISTORY ON command. You can also turn off the HISTORY feature with the SET HISTORY OFF command.

The LIST HISTORY command will display all the lines available without pausing. The number of lines being listed may be limited to the number specified by the LAST keyword. You may also indicate that the display is to be printed.

The LIST MEMORY command

Syntax: LIST MEMORY [TO PRINT]

The LIST MEMORY command is used to look at the contents of active memory variables. It lists the names, types and contents of memory variables. In the dBASE III specification you may add the TO PRINT clause to send the details to the printer. In dBASE II the same effect may be obtained by using the SET PRINT ON command before issuing the LIST MEMORY command. Clipper does not support the LIST MEMORY command, but the same function is available in the separate debugger utility that accompanies the compiler.

The LIST STATUS command

Syntax: LIST STATUS [TO PRINT]

The LIST STATUS command is used to find out which database files and indexes are currently in USE, the current settings of the on/off kind of SET commands, and so on. One of the most useful features of this command is the fact that it displays the keys of all active index files, as in the following dBASE III example:

```
. list status
Currently selected database:
Select area - 1, Database in use: C:motor.dbf
    Index file: C:cars.ndx  key - make+model
    Index file: C:cost.ndx  key - value
```

In the dBASE III specification you may add the TO PRINT clause to send the details to the printer. In dBASE II the same effect may be obtained by using the SET PRINT ON command before issuing the LIST STATUS command. Clipper does not support the LIST STATUS command, but the same function is available in the separate debugger utility that accompanies the compiler.

If you are working at the screen, the DISPLAY STATUS command is preferable to the LIST STATUS command since the former pauses in the course of producing the listing.

The LIST STRUCTURE command

Syntax: LIST STRUCTURE [TO PRINT]

The LIST STRUCTURE command, as its name implies, shows the structure of the database file currently in USE:

```
Structure for database : C:motor.dbf
Number of data records :     178
Date of last update    : 12/12/86
Field  Field name  Type        Width    Dec
    1  MAKE        Character     10
    2  MODEL       Character      8
    3  USER        Character     17
    4  VALUE       Numeric        9       2
    5  YEAR        Numeric        2
    6  NOTES       Memo          10
    7  MILES       Numeric        5
    8  LASTDATE    Date           8
** Total **                      70
```

It also shows the number of records and the date the database file was last changed.

In the dBASE III specification you may add the TO PRINT clause to send the details to the printer. In dBASE II the same effect may be obtained by using the SET PRINT ON command before issuing the LIST STRUCTURE command. Clipper does not support the LIST STRUCTURE command. LIST STRUCTURE is identical to DISPLAY STRUCTURE except that it will show all fields without pause.

The LOAD command

Syntax: LOAD filename

The LOAD command is used by dBASE III PLUS to load an external program routine, in the form of a binary file, into memory where it can be executed with the CALL command. A binary file may be created from a .EXE file by means of the DOS EXE2BIN utility program. Note that the external routine should return to dBASE at the end of its execution, not to the operating system. This means that you should not use routines which were converted from an .EXE file that ends with an exit call: the correct method of exiting is with a FAR return. Also, you should ensure that the first executable instruction is ORGed to an offset of zero, that the CS (code segment) and SS (stack segment) registers are restored before the routine is exited, and that the size of any variable passed to the routine is not changed.

dBASE III PLUS allows you to load up to five binary files at a time, each to a maximum of 32K bytes. If you do not supply a filename extension, the extension of .BIN will be assumed. If you intend to use the RUN command in a program that uses the LOAD command, the externally RUN program will overwrite the loaded binary file unless you set a different MAXMEM value in the CONFIG.DB file. This should be equal to 256K bytes plus the aggregate size of your loaded modules. The RELEASE MODULE command may be used to remove a loaded file from memory. The LOAD command is not included with the Clipper compiler since external modules are linked into the application, not loaded at run time.

The LOCATE command

Syntax: LOCATE [scope] FOR condition

The purpose of this command is to search the database file for a record that matches the condition specified in the FOR clause. If the scope is not specified, the search will start at the beginning of the database file, otherwise it will start at the current record. The SCOPE clause allows you to limit the command, for example by specifying the NEXT one or more records.

The FOR clause specifies the condition(s) under which the search is to be conducted. As soon as a record is found which satisfies the specified conditions, the operation of the LOCATE command stops. This record will now be the current record which means that any of the commands such as DISPLAY, REPLACE, and so forth, which act on the current record, may next be used.

Any of the comparison methods described under the DISPLAY command may be used in the FOR clause of the LOCATE command. If a record matching the specified conditions is not found, the current record will be the last record in the file and the end of file condition will be set. However, if the NEXT clause has been employed, the current record after an unsuccessful LOCATE will be the last record included in the scope clause.

The advantage of the LOCATE command is that you do not need to have an index in place to use the command, as you would with either FIND or SEEK. You could thus initiate an unplanned or arbitrary search and still establish whether or not the database contains the required information. At the same time, such a search would be slow because it might need to read through the entire database before coming up with a yes or no answer. Generally, an indexed lookup such as that provided by the FIND or SEEK commands is preferable to the LOCATE command. By the way, if you do intend to use the LOCATE command in this way, it will operate much faster on a database file which does not have an index SET or in USE. (See also the CONTINUE command.)

The LOOP command

Syntax: LOOP

The purpose of this command is to avoid execution of the remainder of a DO loop by transferring control back to the beginning of the DO loop. It is usually found in an IF...ENDIF group of commands following a tested condition which categorically means that none of the subsequent tests or actions in the DO loop will be required. It has a similar application to the EXIT command, in that both avoid the execution of subsequent commands within the DO loop except that the EXIT command transfers control to a point past the DO loop, i.e. it leaves the loop.

Purists of the structural programming method frown on the use of devices such as the LOOP command, believing the ELSE command to be the correct alternative. The real reason for the LOOP command in dBASE is to save interpreter time. In a compiled application, where control would be transferred immediately to the point past the ELSE group of commands, there would be no need for such a command.

Take care to use the LOOP command correctly: it will always refer to the most recent DO command which may not be the one you had in mind, particularly if you are using nested loops, i.e. loops within loops.

The MENU TO command

Syntax: MENU TO memory variable

This is a Clipper compiler command which is used in conjunction with the @ PROMPT command, as in the following example:

```
Set Message To 23
a 21,11 Prompt ' Next '       Message ':- Display Next Record.'
a 21,24 Prompt ' Previous '   Message ':- Display Previous Record.'
a 21,40 Prompt ' Edit Memo '  Message ':- Edit The Text in The Box.'
a 21,57 Prompt ' Quit '       Message ':- Leave Example Program.'
Menu To Menu1
*
Do Case
  Case (Menu1 = 0)  .OR. (Menu1 = 4)
    Close Data
    Quit
    *
  Case Menu1 = 1
    Skip
```

The string following the PROMPT keyword is displayed at the specified row,column coordinates, while the string following the Message keyword is displayed on the row specified in the SET MESSAGE TO command. The screen appearance of the example above would be as follows:

```
    Next          Previous        Edit Memo        Quit
```

```
  :- Display Next Record.
```

The MENU TO command will highlight the first prompt, at the same time displaying the associated message contained in the @ PROMPT command on the specified message line. If you move to the next prompt by means of the right arrow key, it will be highlighted and the message on the message line will change to that specified in the second @ PROMPT command.

A prompt, i.e. a menu option, may be selected by pressing the Return key, or either of the PgUp or PgDn keys. The MENU TO command is similar to the READ command in that the relative number of the selected prompt will be stored in the variable specified by the MENU TO command. A value of zero means that the Escape key has been pressed. The commands that follow the MENU TO command will be similar to those that follow a READ command in menu processing, for example the CASE command may be used to select an appropriate course of action depending on the prompt selected. Up to 32 prompts, i.e. 32 @ PROMPT command lines, may be given with a single MENU TO command. The prompts do not have to appear side by side as in the example: any of the usual row,column coordinates are acceptable.

The MODIFY COMMAND command

Syntax: MODIFY COMMAND filename

This command is used as the internal dBASE editor, mainly to create and edit dBASE programs, but it may be used with any type of text file. A file extension of .PRG is assumed if no extension is supplied (.CMD in CP/M versions of dBASE II).

In dBASE II the editor is very rudimentary and most users prefer to use external editors such as WordStar or SideKick. The WordStar RUN command allows you to execute dBASE II from within WordStar so that you do not need to return to DOS in between editing and executing your dBASE program.

The CTRL and R feature of WordStar even saves you the bother of typing in the filename of your dBASE program on a second or subsequent edit. Remember, however, to use the N command for editing programs in WordStar, not the D command. The latter marks ends of words with an extra bit set in the corresponding bytes, and this disturbs other programs such as the dBASE products when they read the file.

SideKick is a great favourite with programmers since it resides in memory, which makes it possible to flick between the execution of a program and the editing of the same program at the touch of a key. Bear in mind that dBASE II, dBASE III and FoxBASE are all interpreters, so you may change the program even as you are executing it. Remember, however, that SideKick changes the program on disk, not in dBASE memory: it is necessary to get dBASE to reread the program file, for example by returning to a point in the program earlier than the DO command which reads the program file.

The dBASE III editor is more sophisticated than that in dBASE II, for example it allows you to read in external programs or files to the file you are editing, but it is nonetheless not entirely satisfactory. One of its main drawbacks is not having a facility whereby lines of the program may be moved or copied within the program while editing it. Its main value lies in being able to make quick changes without leaving dBASE III, but even here the features of SideKick described above represent an improvement.

You may, by the way, use an alternative editor within dBASE III by specifying the name of the editor in the CONFIG.DB file which is read by dBASE III as it loads. When you issue the MODIFY COMMAND

command, the specified editor will be loaded instead: it is equivalent to calling it with the dBASE III RUN command, and it will require extra memory on top of that used by dBASE III itself.

Being a compiler, Clipper does not have an editor, so you would use your preferred editor in creating or changing your dBASE programs. If you are using dBASE III to develop your application, you might use MODIFY COMMAND. In the context of the latter, you should be aware that the dBASE III editor will automatically wrap a line that exceeds 66 characters, by leaving soft carriage return characters at the end of a wrapped line and moving the excess to the line below. If you want the line to be a long one you can unwrap it, for example with CTRL and T. However, if you leave it wrapped, Clipper will read it as two separate lines and probably signal a syntax error. I believe a utility program is available to unwrap such lines.

The MODIFY STRUCTURE command

Syntax: MODIFY STRUCTURE

The MODIFY STRUCTURE command is used to change the layout of a database file until it reflects your latest requirements. In the dBASE II specification you will lose the contents of the database, so you have to ensure that you create a copy of the database before you start.

In dBASE III itself a copy of your existing database file will be created for you, using the same filename but replacing the extension .DBF with .BAK. It will then use this copy file as input and write to your new structure as much of the information as it is able to. If you have simply added fields or enlarged the size of fields, dBASE III will transfer all your old information. It will also manage to perform the transfer if you change the name of a field provided you do not change the original position of the field (or the field length) as well. Character fields that are larger than the new field will be truncated, while those that are smaller will be padded out with trailing spaces. Numeric fields are treated according to content. If the size of a numeric field on the new structure is too small to take the value contained in a numeric field of a specific record, the transfer will not succeed for that record and the field will be set to asterisks.

The CREATE utility supplied with the Clipper compiler to create new database files is also used to modify the structure of existing database files. This utility does not create a .BAK copy of the file, so you should ensure that you have a copy of the file before you start. Afterwards you would use the APPEND FROM command to reload the database from the copy you have taken.

The NOTE command

Syntax: NOTE   explanatory text
        *   explanatory text

The NOTE or * command allows you to place comments in your program, or simply to space out the lines of a program to improve its legibility, for example:

```
Clear
*
a 3,5 Say 'Name & Dept'
a 3,21 Say Surname
a 3,32 Say Dept
*
Do While .T.
  Set Color To /w,w/
  a 7,15 Say Oldsalary
  Set Color To w+/,/w
  *
```

See also the && command for placing comments on the same lines as commands.

The ON command

Syntax: ON ERROR command line
       ON ESCAPE command line
       ON KEY   command line

The ON command was introduced by dBASE III PLUS. It allows you to trap a specified event and execute a command line, usually a command that executes a procedure which can deal with the event. There are three events which may be trapped:

● a dBASE error has occurred
● the Escape key has been pressed
● any key has been pressed

The command line specified by the ON command is not executed until the event takes place. For this reason, ON ERROR commands are usually issued at the start of a program to ensure that the application is ready to trap any errors that might occur. Let us look at an example:

```
on error do errdisp
use cars index cars
    .
    .
    .

procedure errdisp
clear
? "The following error has occurred. Please contact the support desk."
?
? "Error number ",error()
? message()
return
```

The dotted lines in the example above represent the bulk of the dBASE program. The RETURN command will pass execution back to the point in the program where the event occurred, thus to the command following that which was interrupted. An ON command may be placed anywhere in a program and may be cancelled by issuing a further ON command of the same type, for example another ON ERROR, which does not specify a command line.

The ON ESCAPE command will trap the use of the Escape key unless the SET ESCAPE OFF command has been issued. The purpose of the ON ESCAPE event trap is to allow a user to press the Escape key when necessary, but to take control when they do so instead of returning them to the dot prompt which is the normal result of pressing this key. You may, for example, allow the use of the Escape key to interrupt a long printed listing.

The ON KEY event will cause an interruption when *any* key is pressed. However, it will wait until the command that is currently in process has been completed. If this is a long-winded operation such as LIST or INDEX, the interruption will nevertheless not take place until after the command has finished. If you want to create an interruption as soon as the key is pressed, you should tell the user to use the Escape key. Either the ON ESCAPE or ON KEY commands will trap the Escape key if it is pressed, but in the latter case you should test for it yourself by using the INKEY( ) function.

The ON KEY command does not itself look at the key that was pressed: it expects the program to examine it by removing the character from the keyboard buffer by means of the INKEY( ) function or commands such as WAIT TO and READ. Indeed, if you do not remove the character, the ON KEY event will repeat itself without any further keys having been pressed. If both the ON KEY and the ON ESCAPE commands have been issued, pressing the Escape key will activate the

ON ESCAPE event but if ON ESCAPE has not been issued (and if SET ESCAPE is OFF), the Escape key will activate the ON KEY event.

See the SET KEY command for a Clipper equivalent to the ON KEY and ON ESCAPE commands.

The PACK command

Syntax: PACK

While the DELETE command is used to mark records that are to be removed from the database file, the PACK command carries out the physical deletion.

At the beginning of each record in the database is one character that is used by the DELETE command to set the deletion marker. The same character is used by the PACK command to tell it to remove the record from the database. Until the PACK command is issued, such records may be retrieved by using the RECALL command.

The PACK command rewrites the database by moving records up towards the beginning of the database, overwriting records marked for deletion. This means that the physical location or record number of all records which follow a deleted record will be changed so that all indexes which relate to the databases will subsequently be invalid.

For this reason, the PACK command recreates all active index files, i.e. those named by the most recent USE or SET INDEX TO commands. It obtains the index key for each of these indexes from the index files themselves and performs exactly as the INDEX command would have done had you reissued it. In this respect the PACK command is simply invoking the REINDEX command.

The PARAMETERS command

Syntax: PARAMETERS parameter list

The PARAMETERS command is used in a called program module to receive memory variables which have been passed in the WITH clause of the calling DO command. Let us look at the following example:

```
* SPHERE.PRG
set talk off
clear
? 'SPHERE VOLUME CALCULATION'
?
input 'Enter radius of the circle ' to radius
store 0 to vol
do volume with radius,vol
?
? 'The sphere volume is ',vol
?
wait
clear
return



* VOLUME.PRG
parameters r,v
x = r*r*r
v = 4/3*3.14159*x
return
```

The PARAMETERS command must be the first executable command in the called program. In our example, the first command is PARAMETERS, which specifies two memory variables corresponding to those passed by the calling program, albeit not with the same names as those being passed to it. You will also notice that the VOLUME program does not create the variable R; it simply uses it. This is because it is assigned a local variable name by the PARAMETER command. Since the variable names do not coincide, the only relationship between the two sets of variables is their relative position in the WITH list and the PARAMETER list, i.e. the contents of the first WITH variable will be related to the first variable specified in the PARAMETER list, and so on.

Parameters can be passed by value or by reference. If the parameter being passed is an expression, the value of the expression is evaluated and passed to be placed in a local variable. If the parameter is the name of a memory variable it is passed by reference, i.e. the value is used from the variable in the calling program. Such a variable may be changed by the called module, even though it is using the locally assigned name, and the change will be effective in the calling program. The following illustrates this point:

```
clear all
store 2 to height,width,length
store 0 to cube
do cubecalc with height,length,width,cube
disp memo
return

procedure cubecalc
para w,x,y,z
z = w*x*y
store 9 to w
disp memo
return
```

The first memory display, i.e. that contained in the called procedure, looks like this:

```
HEIGHT      priv (hidden) N          9
WIDTH       priv (hidden) N          2
LENGTH      priv (hidden) N          2
CUBE        priv (hidden) N          8
W               priv @ HEIGHT
X               priv @ LENGTH
Y               priv @ WIDTH
Z               priv @ CUBE
```

As you can see, the cube was correctly calculated using a height of 2, and the contents of the variable HEIGHT in the calling program were then changed to another value. The memory display in the calling program confirms the change:

```
HEIGHT      priv N          9
WIDTH       priv N          2
LENGTH      priv N          2
CUBE        priv N          8
```

The PRIVATE command

Syntax: PRIVATE memory variable(s)
          PRIVATE [ALL] [ALL LIKE skeleton]
              [ALL EXCEPT skeleton]

The PRIVATE command is used to allow sharing of memory variable names, so that a variable in a called module may have the same name as a variable in the calling module without disturbing the latter. What happens is that any variables that already exist when the called module is entered, and with names stipulated by the PRIVATE command, will be temporarily hidden until the called module ends. Let us look at the following example:

```
clear all
store 2 to height,width,length
store 0 to cube
do ptest
return
     .

     .

procedure ptest
private height,width,length
store 43 to height,width,length
disp memo
return
```

The memory display below shows clearly that there are two variables each with the names HEIGHT, WIDTH, and LENGTH, although containing different values. It also shows that the set of the three variables created in the calling module is hidden.

```
HEIGHT       priv (hidden)  N          2
WIDTH        priv (hidden)  N          2
LENGTH       priv (hidden)  N          2
CUBE         priv  N               0
HEIGHT       priv  N              43
WIDTH        priv  N              43
LENGTH       priv  N              43
```

This means that the contents of such variables cannot be affected by commands within the called module, even where these have been declared as PUBLIC elsewhere in the program. Note too that the CUBE variable is not hidden and may therefore be altered by the called module. When the called module ends, all variables it has created will be released and any variables named in the PRIVATE command will revert to their original status.

The ALL, ALL LIKE, or ALL EXCEPT clauses may be used instead of a list of named variables in dBASE III but not in Clipper. The dBASE II specification does not support the PRIVATE command.

The PROCEDURE command

Syntax: PROCEDURE procedure name

The PROCEDURE command identifies the beginning of a procedure or routine in a procedure file. In dBASE III and dBASE III PLUS a procedure file is simply a .PRG file which contains more than one program module, up to a maximum of 32. The procedure file is activated by the SET PROCEDURE TO command, and thereafter it will be searched for a program module whenever the DO command is executed. If the module called by the DO command is not found in the procedure file, dBASE will look for it in the usual way on the default disk drive. The Clipper compiler allows you to include procedures at the foot of the calling .PRG file instead of in a separate file. The dBASE II specification does not support procedures.

The PUBLIC command

Syntax: PUBLIC memory variable(s)
       PUBLIC CLIPPER

The PUBLIC command is used to prevent the release of specified memory variables when the program module in which they are created comes to an end. In the dBASE III specification, memory variables created within a command file are non-global, which means that they do not exist outside the program module that created them unless it is within a nested program module, i.e. one that was called from within the module which created the variable. When a program module is terminated, all memory variables created by that module are released. If, within a program, you do want to declare a memory variable global you have to do so deliberately by using the PUBLIC command. This command specifies a list of the memory variables that you want to declare as public, but with one important condition: you have to declare the variable as public before you use it in a STORE command or other command that initialises it.

The second form of the PUBLIC command is used to include Clipper specific or dBASE III specific commands in a program that will run under either. The following example explains its use:

```
public clipper
if clipper
  @ 5,5,25,75 box ""
else
  @ 5,5 clear to 25,75
endif
```

With one exception, a PUBLIC memory variable will test as logically False in an IF command. The exception is a variable called CLIPPER when used in a Clipper compiled program, where it will return logical

True. In the example above, used in dBASE III, the variable CLIPPER when tested will return a logical False so that the @ TO command following the ELSE will be executed. The @ TO command, of course, is supported only by dBASE III PLUS not by Clipper. If the same example was used in a Clipper compiled program, the IF command would return a logical True so that the @ BOX command (unique to Clipper) would be used instead. Both @ commands in the example will clear a box drawn on the screen, but one is Clipper specific while the other is dBASE III PLUS specific.

The PUBLIC command is not supported in the dBASE II specification.

The QUIT command

Syntax: QUIT

The QUIT command closes all open files, ends the dBASE session and returns control to the operating system.

The READ command

Syntax: READ [SAVE]

The READ command is used to activate a GET area and to transfer data from the GET area, i.e. from the screen area specified by the GET clause of the @ command. The @ GET command does no more than display a variable or field on the screen. If you do not issue the READ command, nothing else will happen. It is the READ command that activates the cursor in the GET area and enables you to enter or change data, and which moves the data from the GET area to the memory variable or database field specified in the @ GET command.

The READ command will activate all @ GETs issued since the previous READ or CLEAR GETS command. Note that the CLEAR and CLEAR ALL commands will also clear GETS. If you add the SAVE clause to the READ command, it will not clear the GETS. This means that you can redisplay the GETS simply by reissuing the READ command. If the GETS are displaying fields direct from a database record, they will always reflect the contents of the current record even where the SAVE clause has been used.

The RECALL command

Syntax: RECALL [scope] [FOR/WHILE condition]

The RECALL command is used to reinstate records which have been tagged for deletion by the DELETE command, provided that the PACK command has not already physically removed the records.

At the beginning of each record in the database is one character that is used by the DELETE command to set the deletion marker. This character is used by the PACK command to tell it that the record should be removed from the database. What the RECALL command does is remove the deletion marker.

The scope clauses allow you to limit the RECALL command, for example by specifying the NEXT one or more records, or by using the RECORD clause to delete a specific record. The FOR/WHILE clauses allow you to impose conditions on the records to be processed in the course of the RECALL command. Used on its own the RECALL command will remove the deletion marker of the current record only.

The REINDEX command

Syntax: REINDEX

The REINDEX command recreates all active index files, i.e. those named by the most recent USE or SET INDEX TO commands. It obtains the index key for each of these indexes from the index files themselves and performs exactly as the INDEX command would have done had you reissued it.

The index files are rebuilt one at a time, so that the REINDEX command will read through the complete database file once for each index file to be recreated. The current UNIQUE setting will be ignored since the REINDEX command will duplicate the setting in force at the time the index was originally created.

In dBASE II, the REINDEX command is only valid as from version 2.4.

The RELEASE command

Syntax: RELEASE variable list [ALL]
           [ALL LIKE/EXCEPT skeleton]

This command deletes memory variables from memory. In its simplest form just one or two variables are released:

```
release reply,option
```

If you want to delete all memory variables starting with the letters CA, you would employ a skeleton as follows:

```
release all like ca*
```

Finally, you can delete memory variables indiscriminately with the ALL clause:

```
release all
```

In the dBASE II specification this form of the RELEASE command will delete every single variable in memory. In the dBASE III specification it will release only those which were created in the sub-program in which the command is being issued. Variables created at higher levels will not be affected.

The RELEASE MODULE command

Syntax: RELEASE MODULE filename

This dBASE III PLUS command removes a binary file that was read into memory by the LOAD command, and releases the memory occupied by the loaded file. The filename is that specified by the corresponding LOAD command.

The REMARK command

Syntax: REMARK text

The REMARK command appears only in the dBASE II specification. It allows you to display the text that follows the REMARK keyword. The text may be directed at the printer if the SET PRINT ON command has been issued previously. The REMARK command may be seen as a limited version of the TEXT command.

The RENAME command

Syntax: RENAME current filename TO new filename

The RENAME command changes the name of a disk file. Any type of file may be renamed but the filename extension must be included, even when it is a database file.

The REPLACE command

Syntax: REPLACE [scope] field WITH expression
[FOR/WHILE condition]

The REPLACE command is used to change the contents of database fields in the database file currently in USE. In dBASE programs it is typically used to update a single database record, for example after an APPEND BLANK command or after the database fields have been displayed and changed by the combination of @ GET and READ commands. More than one field may be replaced in a single command, for example:

```
replace make with makex, model with modelx, cost with costx
```

If the SCOPE, FOR, or WHILE clauses are included, REPLACE may be used to change the contents of several database records starting with the current record. The SCOPE clause allows you to limit the command, for example by specifying the NEXT one or more records. The FOR/WHILE clauses allow you to impose conditions on the records to be processed in the course of the REPLACE command. You may, for example, update a price in each record in a given sales area by an increase of 10%:

```
replace price with price*1.1 for area = "NE"
```

If the SCOPE or FOR/WHILE clauses are not specified, REPLACE will operate on the current record only. Otherwise it will move through the database file either in record number sequence or, if an index is active, in the sequence specified by the index file, repositioning the current record pointer as it does so. When working with an index file you should take care not to change the contents of any of the key fields used to create this index file because the current record pointer will immediately jump to the new position in the indexed sequence.

On an individual field the replacement rules are as follows:

1. The field and expression specified in the WITH clause must be of the same type.
2. Character expressions that are larger than the database field will be truncated, while those that are smaller will be padded out with trailing spaces.
3. If the size of a numeric field is too small to take the value contained in the numeric expression, the field will be set to asterisks (dBASE III) or zeros (dBASE II).
4. Memo fields cannot be used in a REPLACE command in dBASE III

or dBASE III PLUS. However, see also the MEMOEDIT function in Chapter 6.

The REPORT command

Syntax: REPORT FORM filename [scope] [FOR/WHILE condition]
[TO PRINT] [TO FILE filename] [PLAIN]
[HEADING string] [NOEJECT] [SUMMARY]

The REPORT command operates on a .FRM file which contains the definition of the report to be produced by the REPORT command. The .FRM file is created either by the REPORT command itself in the dBASE II specification, the CREATE REPORT or MODIFY REPORT commands in dBASE III, or the REPORT utility of Clipper. The awkwardness with the dBASE II method is that it does not allow you to change the definition once you have created it. (The dBASE II report creation is not explained here but it follows a similar approach to that described in the CREATE REPORT pages, except that a question and answer method is followed).

The REPORT command will interpret the definition specified in the filename of the FORM clause and produce a tabular report according to instructions contained in the definition and using database records according to the SCOPE clause and the FOR/WHILE conditions. Page numbers and the system date will automatically be supplied in the page heading:

```
Page No.       1
12/16/86
               LIST OF VEHICLES BY USER


User                Vehicle               Value


Roberts, A G        BMW 316               7614.00
MacKenzie,P         BMW 320i              9370.00
Smart,W R           Mercedes 200TC       11070.00
Kenning,L P         Volvo 360GLT          6700.00
James,H J           Peugeot 305GR         6370.00
Hemmings,K G        Lancia 2000IE         7900.00
Richards,P G        BMW 735i             19750.00
Johnson,H L         Mercedes 380SEL      23670.00
Andrews,J H         BMW 323i             10320.00
*** Total ***

                                        102764.00
```

If you do not want the page numbering or date you may avoid these by including the PLAIN clause in the REPORT command. This will also cause the report heading itself to be printed on the first page only.

The heading is specified in the .FRM file but may be augmented with a runtime heading supplied by the SET HEADING TO command in the dBASE II specification, or the HEADING clause in the dBASE III specification. In the latter instance, the heading should be enclosed in quote marks or square brackets to identify it as a character string.

The SCOPE clause allows you to limit the command, for example by specifying the number of records (starting at the current record) to be processed with the NEXT clause.

Remember, if you have specified sub-totals, that the database file has to be in a logical sequence: either indexed or sorted to the sequence specified in the sub-total control field(s).

If the words TO PRINT are included in the command or the SET PRINT ON command has been issued previously, the details will also appear on the printer. In the dBASE III specification, the details may be written as print lines to a text file by using the TO FILE clause followed by a filename. The filename will be suffixed with the extension .TXT unless you supply your own extension.

Normally the REPORT command, when directed at a printer, will cause a page throw to ensure that the report starts on a new page. In the dBASE III specification, the clause NOEJECT specifies that there should be no paper throw before starting to print the report. In the dBASE II specification it is necessary to issue the SET EJECT OFF command to achieve the same thing.

The SUMMARY clause may be used in dBASE III PLUS to suppress printing the detail lines, i.e. only sub-totals will be printed. Note too that most of the clauses that have been described here, such as NOEJECT, PLAIN, and so forth, may be specified when the report format is being created or modified.

The RESTORE command

Syntax: RESTORE FROM filename [ADDITIVE]

The RESTORE command performs the opposite function to that of the SAVE command: it reads a .MEM disk file and returns to memory the variables contained in the disk file. These variables will, of course, contain the data they had when they were saved. They will also overwrite all the variables already in existence unless you specify the ADDITIVE clause and even then variables of a like name will be overwritten.

The RESTORE SCREEN command

Syntax: RESTORE SCREEN

The Clipper only SAVE SCREEN and RESTORE SCREEN commands are used in conjunction with operations which overwrite the screen temporarily, for example HELP screens. The SAVE SCREEN command does exactly what it says; it creates a copy of the display on the screen. When you issue the RESTORE SCREEN command, the screen that has most recently been saved will be restored. These commands are typically used in conjunction with the context specific help features of the Clipper compiler, but may be used with any routines which want to superimpose text on a screen for a short duration.

The RESUME command

Syntax: RESUME

This dBASE III PLUS command is used in debugging a program and is coupled with the SUSPEND command. SUSPEND stops the program and returns control to the dot prompt where you can execute commands interactively until you want the program to continue execution. Then you issue the RESUME command and the program will carry on from the command line following the SUSPEND command. All current memory variables, including those which are not PUBLIC, will be intact during the period of suspension so that you can carry on using them or examine them with the DISPLAY MEMORY command. Before issuing the RESUME command you should clear the screen with the CLEAR command, otherwise your interactive displays will remain on the screen when your program continues execution.

The RETRY command

Syntax: RETRY

This dBASE III PLUS command is similar to the RETURN command in that it closes the current command file and returns control to the calling program. However, instead of executing the line following the DO command in the calling program, it re-executes the DO command itself, thereby repeating execution of the command file that contains the RETRY command.

The RETRY command is typically used in error recovery when you want to repeat execution of a routine a fixed number of times or until it is successfully completed.

The RETURN command

Syntax: RETURN
             RETURN TO MASTER

The RETURN command hands execution back to the calling module. In the dBASE II specification it also releases all variables created in the module that is being ended, unless they were declared as PUBLIC. Where the structure of a module takes the form of a permanent DO WHILE loop, the RETURN command is often used as the means of breaking out of the loop in order to return control to the calling module. RETURN TO MASTER will return control not to the calling module but to the highest level module. RETURN TO MASTER is not available in dBASE II, nor is it supported in Clipper.

If the RETURN command is encountered in the highest level module, it cancels execution of the dBASE program and returns control to the software that initiated the dBASE program. In the case of dBASE II, FoxBASE, or dBASE III, this will be the interpreter, i.e. to the dot prompt. In the case of a compiled program, i.e. a stand alone .EXE program, control will be returned to the operating system.

The RUN command

Syntax: RUN   command
         !   command

Available only in the dBASE III specification, the RUN or ! command may be used to execute external programs or operating system commands without leaving the dBASE program. RUN does not remove the dBASE program from memory; it calls the external program into spare memory. If there is insufficient memory to load the external program, a message to this effect will be displayed and program execution will continue with the next dBASE command. The RUN command itself adds an overhead of 17 Kbytes plus the memory required by the external program.

In interactive mode, the RUN command is useful for calling up programs like WordStar or Xtree. When you exit from the external program, you are returned to the dot prompt. In programs, RUN is ideal for changing directories. The SET DEFAULT TO command applies only to drives not directories, so that you need another method of setting up a default directory, for example:

```
run cd\accounts
```

The SAVE command

Syntax: SAVE TO filename [ALL LIKE/EXCEPT skeleton]

The SAVE command writes memory variables to a disk file which will have the filename extension .MEM unless you include a different extension when you specify the filename in the command line.

Used on its own, all variables will be written to the .MEM file. If you do not want to write all variables to disk, you can use the ALL LIKE or ALL EXCEPT clauses, for example:

```
save to cars all like ca*
```

The skeleton represents a part spelling of the names of the variables to be included (LIKE) or excluded (EXCEPT) when writing them to the disk file. A skeleton may contain an asterisk to indicate several characters or a question mark to indicate a single character. Thus in the example above, all variables starting with the letters 'CA' will be saved.

The saved variables may be retrieved from disk by the RESTORE command.

The SEEK command

Syntax: SEEK expression

Available only in the dBASE III specification, the SEEK command is very similar to the FIND command. It operates on the main index currently in use, searching the index file for a key that matches the expression specified in the command. In many cases this will be a memory variable so that the SEEK command will be operating on the contents of the variable. When it has found a matching key, SEEK will use the record number contained in that index entry to establish the corresponding record as the current record. The whole process takes place within a second or two. Following the SEEK command, the contents of such a record may be accessed by any of the commands which operate on the current record, for example STORE, REPLACE, @ SAY, and so on.

It is, however, necessary to test that the match was successful. This is done by using the EOF( ) or end of file function: if this function returns an answer of True, there has been no match. As an alternative you could use the FOUND( ) function which returns a logical True if there has been a match.

The expression specified in the SEEK command has to correspond to the beginning of the key but may be shorter than the key. Case differences are observed, i.e. an upper-case string will not match on a key which is held in lower-case. A useful method of getting around this restriction is to apply the UPPER( ) function to the key field(s) when creating the index. If you then consistently use an upper-case string in all SEEK commands, the case differences will not matter.

The SELECT command

dBASE II syntax:
    SELECT PRIMARY/SECONDARY
dBASE III syntax:
    SELECT work area/alias

The SELECT command provides the means of moving from one active database to another. In the dBASE II specification, only two active databases are available, and the PRIMARY and SECONDARY keywords are used to move to either the main or alternative work area. In the dBASE III specification, up to 10 work areas may be used. These are either numbered 1 to 10 or indicated by the letters A to J. They may also be given names, known as alias names. Aliases are established when a database file is opened in a work area, for example:

```
use cars index users alias miles1
select 2
use travel index user2 alias miles2
select 1
```

or:

```
use cars index users alias miles1
select b
use travel index user2 alias miles2
select a
```

If an alias is not explicitly declared any one of the following three may be used as an alias:

● the database filename, for example TRAVEL
● the work area number, for example 2
● the work area letter, for example B

Once an alias has been established, you may use it in the SELECT command, for example:

```
select miles2
```

The SELECT command does not affect the position of any of the current record pointers. This means that you can move from one work area to another without disturbing the database file positions. You do not need to be in a particular work area to use one of its fieldnames. To refer to a field from a database that is active in another work area, you prefix the fieldname with the alias:

```
select 2
store a->make to makex
store miles1->model to modelx
```

A memory variable may not be used in the SELECT command to contain the alias unless you use the macro substitute character to convert the command line prior to execution:

```
store "miles1" to alias2
select &alias2
```

The SET commands

Syntax: SET parameter TO condition
          SET parameter ON/OFF

● **SET ALTERNATE TO** is used to specify the name of a disk file to which everything that normally appears on the screen will be written. This includes the user input as well as dBASE output but does not include the results of @ SAY commands or other full screen operations such as APPEND or EDIT. The file will have a .TXT suffix and will be created if it does not already exist. Output to the file may be switched on and off with the SET ALTERNATE ON/OFF command. Details written to the .TXT file may subsequently be included in a word processing document.

● **SET ALTERNATE ON/OFF** is used to switch on or off the facility of writing dBASE output and user input to a specified .TXT file. It requires a SET ALTERNATE TO command to have been issued previously. Default is OFF.

● **SET BELL ON/OFF** is used to turn the alarm bell on or off. When the bell is on you are notified by the bell (a beep, really) when you have reached the end of a field in full screen APPEND or EDIT mode, and dBASE automatically switches to the next field. Touch typists find it useful because they are often not looking at the screen. Others find the constant noise irritating and switch it off. (See also the SET CONFIRM command.) The bell is also used when you have used format characters in a PICTURE field with the @ GET command and the user attempts to enter an illegal character, for example an alphabetic character into a PICTURE '9999" field. Default is ON.

● **SET CARRY ON** is used when in the APPEND or INSERT mode to display details from the previous record entered and is useful in saving you the work of re-entering details which are the same from one record to the next. You may use the Return key or CTRL and X to move past such fields without changing their contents. SET CARRY OFF is issued to cancel the condition. Default is OFF.

● **SET CATALOG TO** creates or activates a Catalog file. The use of Catalog files relies on first activating a .CAT file with the SET CATALOG TO command and then selecting items from that Catalog file by suffixing standard commands with a ?. These commands are ones which use a filename as part of their syntax, for example SET INDEX TO, USE, MODIFY REPORT, and so forth. Thus when you issue the USE ? command, a selection of database files taken from the open Catalog file will be presented, from which you select the one you want. This is a full screen operation. The .CAT file is just another database file and you may examine its contents after opening it with the USE command provided you remember to supply the .CAT filename extension, for example:

```
use accounts.cat
```

● **SET CATALOG OFF** allows you to override the normal condition whereby an open Catalog is updated by commands such as CREATE, index, and CREATE or MODIFY REPORT. Default is ON.

● **SET CENTURY ON** allows you to enter and display the year in its full form, i.e. 1986 instead of just 86, so that an APPEND or EDIT screen will ask you for 04/04/1986 not 04/04/86.Similarly, on displays such as that of the system date, the year will be shown in full:

```
. set century on
. ? date()
04/04/1986
```

Default is OFF.

● **SET COLOR TO** has the following syntax:

SET COLOR TO a,b,c,d

where:

a : standard display
b : enhanced display
c : border
d : background

The standard display is used by all output such as ? and @ SAY operations, while enhanced display is used by @ GET operations. Let us look at an example first and then examine the possible settings:

```
SET COLOR TO R*/B, W/N, B
```

The above will set standard displays to red flashing on blue, enhanced displays to white on black, and the border to blue. An asterisk (*) indicates that the colour is to flash, while a plus (+) indicates a high intensity display. In the first two parameters, the character to the left of the slash (/) indicates the foreground colours and the character to the right of the slash, the background colour. The following table shows the colours that may be used:

Black	:	N or 0
Blue	:	B or 1
Green	:	G or 2
Cyan	:	BG or 3
Red	:	R or 4
Magenta	:	RB or 5
Brown	:	GR or 6
White	:	W or 7

If you want yellow, you would ask for high intensity brown (GR+).

On a monochrome screen SET COLOR TO may be used to set screen attributes such as underlining and reverse video. As an example, let us look at the following which will underline everything being displayed after the SET COLOR command has been issued:

```
set color to u
```

Note that on a Compaq the screen is not considered to be a monochrome screen (it is a monochrome graphics screen) so the underlining and reverse video effects are not available on Compaq models.

SET COLOR TO on its own will reset the screen to the default colours or screen attributes.

● **SET COLOR ON/OFF** switches between colour and monochrome mode on display monitors which provide both. The default is that which is already in operation when you start dBASE.

● **SET CONFIRM ON** may be used when in full screen APPEND or EDIT mode to prevent dBASE from automatically skipping to the next field when the end of the current field has been reached. If you keep typing, the final character will change continuously to reflect what you are entering, but the cursor will not move on to the next field until you have pressed the Return key or used CTRL and X. If the bell is on (see SET BELL) a beep will sound for every character you attempt to enter past the end of the field. Default is OFF.

● **SET CONSOLE ON/OFF** is used to turn the screen on or off as an output device. It can be useful if you want a user to enter a password but do not want to have it appear on the screen. Default is ON.

● **SET DATE** allows you to choose a national date format for both data entry and display. If you select SET DATE BRITISH, then all dates will take the form DD/MM/YY; if you then try to enter a date in the American format, for example 12/24/86, you will get an error. The options are:

BRITISH	:	DD/MM/YY
FRENCH	:	DD/MM/YY
ITALIAN	:	DD-MM-YY
GERMAN	:	DD.MM.YY
AMERICAN	:	MM/DD/YY
ANSI	:	YY.MM.DD

Default is SET DATE AMERICAN.

● **SET DEBUG ON** is a specialised SET PRINT ON command and is used when you are trying to iron out the errors (or bugs) in a command file. You will already be using SET ECHO ON and possibly SET STEP ON, but will want to have the results of those two SET commands displayed on the printer so that they do not clutter up the screen. Default is OFF.

● **SET DECIMALS TO** may be used to specify the precision of the divide operator, and the SQRT, LOG and EXP functions. The number of decimals in the result will normally display as two.

● **SET DEFAULT TO** specifies the drive on which dBASE expects to find files. If it is not used, dBASE expects to find all files on the drive from which the program was loaded.

● **SET DELETED** is used to control the execution of commands in respect of records marked for deletion. If, for example, you have issued the SET DELETED ON command, COUNT will not include any records marked for deletion. Default is OFF.

● **SET DELIMITERS TO** may be used in conjunction with the SET DELIMITERS ON command to provide an alternative way of displaying the field boundaries, for example when you use the @ GET command or any full screen commands such as APPEND. The default method of displaying a field is by reverse video. When SET DELIMITER ON is issued, the character(s) specified in the SET DELIMITER TO command will be used to mark the beginning and end of fields. The reverse video display will also be shown unless the SET INTENSITY OFF command has been issued. The syntax is:

SET DELIMITERS TO character expression/DEFAULT

The DEFAULT keyword sets the delimiter character to the default of colons. If you specify two characters as in the example below, the first will be used as the beginning character and the second as the ending character:

```
set deli to "[]"
```

In dBASE II, colons are displayed by default on either side of the reverse video field.

● **SET DELIMITER ON** may be used to specify an alternative to the reverse video method of displaying a field size in commands like @ GET or APPEND. If SET DELIMITER ON is issued without a preceding SET DELIMITER TO, the default delimiter of colons will be used. Default is OFF.

● **SET DEVICE TO** is used to direct output of @ SAY commands either to the screen or the printer by issuing a SET DEVICE TO SCREEN or SET DEVICE TO PRINT command respectively. Default is TO SCREEN.

● **SET DOHISTORY ON** will cause the DISPLAY HISTORY or LIST HISTORY commands to include command lines executed by a DO command, i.e. those contained in a .PRG file. Default is OFF.

● **SET ECHO ON** is used to display program lines as they are executed to assist you in following the results of the command file. You may direct this output to the printer with the SET DEBUG ON command. Default is OFF.

● **SET ESCAPE ON** permits you to cancel the execution of a command file by pressing the Escape key, whereas the OFF condition will prevent such an escape. Default is ON.

● **SET EXACT ON** is used to specify that an exact match must be made, for example in a FIND command an abbreviated item will not be found. This SET command may similarly specify that a compare operation provides a full match and not just a match on the characters given in the second part of an equation. Default is OFF.

● **SET FIELDS TO** allows you to apply a mask to all active database files whereby you select the fields that can be displayed or entered. The command specifies a list of those fields that are to be active. Used on its own, the command will remove from the active list all fields which are contained in the currently selected database. The opposite to this is SET FIELDS TO ALL, which will add to the active list all the fields contained in the currently selected database. Extra SET FIELDS TO commands do not contradict earlier SET FIELDS TO commands: they add to the list of active fields. The SET FIELDS TO command requires the SET FIELDS ON command to be issued, otherwise the SET FIELDS TO condition will be ignored.

● **SET FIELDS ON** will activate the field selection dictated by the SET FIELDS TO command. Default is OFF.

● **SET FILTER TO** allows you to specify a condition which will filter the database file so that only records that meet the condition appear to exist. The condition is cancelled by reissuing the SET FILTER TO command without a condition. The syntax is:

SET FILTER TO condition

The condition may be any test such as MAKE = 'BMW'. As an alternative, instead of supplying a condition you may use the FILE clause to specify the name of a Query .QRY file:

```
set filter to names
```

The NAMES.QRY file will have been created by the CREATE QUERY command and will contain the condition(s).

● **SET FIXED ON** will force the display of the standard number of decimals on all numeric output. The standard number is either 2 or as set by the SET DECIMALS TO command. Even functions like RECNO( ) will be affected. Default is OFF.

```
. ? recno()
        8
. set fixed on
. ? recno()
        8.00
```

● **SET FORMAT TO** is used to direct commands like READ, APPEND and EDIT to use the contents of an .FMT file.

● **SET FUNCTION TO** is used to reprogram the function keys of the computer other than Function key 1 which is the HELP key. For example Function key 3, which is preset to issue the LIST command, may be changed to issue ACCEPT 'Enter File ' TO name:

```
set function 3 to "accept 'Enter File ' to name;"
```

Notice that the complete command must be enclosed in quotes and if the command itself requires quotes, as in the example, that double quotes may be used for one and single for the other. Note too the semicolon at the end of the ACCEPT command line. This signals that the command is to be executed immediately upon Function key 3 being pressed, without waiting for the Return key to be pressed.

● **SET HEADING ON/OFF** determines whether or not to display fieldnames or expressions as column captions during the display of information by commands like LIST. Default is ON.

● **SET HELP ON/OFF** is used to allow or suppress the 'Do you want some help? (Y/N)' query that displays when you have made a mistake in entering a command. The default is ON.

● **SET HISTORY TO** is used change the number of lines that will be stored as history with the SET HISTORY TO command. The default is 20 lines.

● **SET HISTORY OFF** can be used to turn off the HISTORY feature (see the DISPLAY HISTORY command). Default is ON.

● **SET INDEX TO** is used to set an alternative index or indexes. The specified index(es) will replace those currently in use. The syntax is:

SET INDEX TO list of index filenames

Up to seven index filenames, separated by commas, may be given. The filename extension of .NDX is not necessary. SET INDEX TO on its own will close all active index files. Only the first index file will control the sequence of the information in the database file, but all the indexes will be updated when changes are made to the database.

● **SET INTENSITY ON/OFF** controls the use of inverse video on the screen during the operation of commands like @ GET, APPEND, and so forth. Default is ON.

● **SET KEY** is a Clipper compiler command that is similar to the ON KEY command of dBASE III PLUS, and is used to test for special keys such as Escape, or Insert. The syntax is as follows:

SET KEY numeric expression TO procedure name

SET KEY allows you to associate a procedure with a key value, given by the numeric expression, so that when that key is pressed at any of the wait states listed below, the procedure will be executed:

```
ACCEPT
INPUT
MENU TO
READ
WAIT
```

A list of key values is given in Chapter 6 in the description of the INKEY( ) function. The associated procedure must begin with a PARAMETERS command which accepts the following three parameters:

● a character variable containing the name of the calling program
● a numeric variable containing the source code line number of the command that initiated the wait condition
● a character variable containing the name of the memory variable that is waiting for user input

The RETURN command at the end of the procedure will return control to the point at which the key was pressed, i.e. to the command which caused the wait condition. Depending on the key that was pressed the procedure may, of course, choose to abort the program instead or pass control to some other section of the program.

Clipper compiled programs also have automatic help support which is based on the SET KEY format. Clipper provides an automatic SET KEY for the F1 function key in such a way that a call is made to a procedure called HELP or a program file called HELP.PRG when the F1 key is pressed. The content of the HELP procedure is up to the programmer but, since you can tell which module was in operation when the F1 key was called, you are in a position to display context specific help messages. You could, for example, access another database file containing all the valid options for a particular @ GET, such as valid sales area codes, and display a list of these.

● **SET MARGIN TO** provides a user control over the positioning of printed output. All print lines will be moved to the right by the number of positions specified.

● **SET MEMOWIDTH TO** is used to change the column width of Memo fields during a display operation. Normally this is set to 50 characters wide.

● **SET MENU** controls whether the cursor control menu automatically appears for APPEND, EDIT, MODIFY COMMAND, and other full screen commands. The default is OFF which means that you have to press Function key 1 to obtain the menu. When the SET MENU ON command has been issued, you can use Function key 1 to stop the display of the menu.

● **SET MESSAGE TO** in dBASE III PLUS allows you to choose your own message that will be displayed during full screen operations such as APPEND and EDIT.
SET MESSAGE TO is also a Clipper command that is part of its menu processing features. It is used to define a row or line number for messages contained in @ PROMPT commands. Please refer to the description of the latter for an explantion.

● **SET ORDER TO** allows you to change the controlling index file without closing and opening all the index files by means of a SET INDEX TO command. If you want to set as controlling index file the index which is currently second in the list specified by the USE command or the SET INDEX TO command, you would issue the command as follows:

```
set order to 2
```

If you want to select the physical sequence of records in the database file, you would select a file of zero:

```
set order to 0
```

When you issue the SET ORDER TO command, the current record pointer remains undisturbed. This also means that you should issue a

GO TOP command or similar if it is necessary to set the current record pointer to the beginning of the indexed sequence.

● **SET PATH TO** directs dBASE to alternate DOS directories in trying to find files that it cannot find in the current directory:

```
set path to \banks
```

The syntax is:

SET PATH TO path list

If you want to specify more than one path, the pathnames are separated by commas. You may, of course, direct dBASE to perform all its processing in another directory by using the dBASE RUN command to issue the DOS change directory (CD or CHDIR) command.

● **SET PRINT ON** directs dBASE output to the printer as well as to the screen. It does not include the output from @ SAY commands for which you have to issue the SET DEVICE TO PRINT command. Default is OFF.

● **SET PRINTER TO** allows you to select a DOS device for printer output. Normally all printer output will be directed to the standard DOS device of LPT1. You may, however, want to redirect your printer output to a serial port such as COM1, for example if you have a laser printer with a serial interface. The available options with this command are:

```
LPT1
LPT2
LPT3
COM1
COM2
```

The first three are for parallel connection, the last two for serial connection.

● **SET PROCEDURE TO** is used to designate a file that contains a dBASE procedure. It is used in partnership with the PROCEDURE command.

● **SET RELATION TO** is used to link active database files in different work areas so that movement on one will automatically cause movement on the others to corresponding records. This is an important feature of relational database software and is used to ensure that two or more database files are in step with one another so that information can be assembled from all the related database files. For example, if you have an Invoice file and an Order file, both of which relate to your customers, you will not want to duplicate the customer name and address on each invoice record and each order record for the same customer. Instead you will have a Customer file containing the name and address and simply relate the Invoice and Order files to the Customer file. The method of relating is by supplying a common key, for example a customer code. Provided the related files are indexed on this key, it is a simple matter for dBASE to see to it that the current record in each file represents that key. It does so by means of the SET RELATION TO command.

What happens is that the contents of the field specified by the TO clause of the SET RELATION TO command are used to execute an internal FIND on the other databases, which explains why the latter have to be indexed. There is no need to have the same fieldname in all the related databases since it is the *field contents* that are used to FIND the corresponding records. This also means that, just as with the FIND command itself, you do not have to provide the full key. Thus a customer code of HEND will successfully find a record containing HENDERSON in the related file provided the related file is indexed on the field containing the name HENDERSON. The syntax has more than one format, but let us look at the obvious one first:

SET RELATION TO fieldname INTO alias

The ALIAS identifies another database (called the child) in an active work area, while the FIELDNAME represents the key field in the first database (called the Parent), for example:

```
use invoices
select 2
use customer index custno
select 1
set relation to custcode into b
list invno,invdate,custcode,b->name
```

To relate more files, i.e. more children to the same parent, you repeat the TO/INTO clause:

```
use invoices
select 2
use customer index custno
select 3
use orders index orderno
select 1
set relation to custcode into b, to ordercode into c
list invno,invdate,custcode,b->name,c->orderval
```

At the time of writing it is possible to use the SET RELATION TO command to relate a maximum of eight child databases to a parent if you use the Clipper compiler, and one child database to a parent if you use dBASE III PLUS.

Two other syntaxes may be used. In place of the FIELDNAME, you may specify RECNO( ) or you may specify a numeric expression. Both will cause the database file specified by the INTO clause to be repositioned to a specific record number as specified either by the RECNO( ) function or the numeric expression. The RECNO( ) function will, of course, return the current record number in the parent database.

● **SET SAFETY** controls whether or not you are told when you are about to overwrite an existing file. If SAFETY is OFF you could, for example, overwrite an existing index file with the INDEX command without any warning. If SAFETY is ON, a warning message will first be displayed. Default is ON.

● **SET SCOREBOARD OFF** may be used to suppress dBASE III messages such as the deletion status of a record, or the insert mode. These normally appear on the status line at the foot of the screen, but if SET STATUS OFF has been issued, they will appear on line 0. Default is ON.

● **SET STATUS OFF** will prevent the display of the dBASE III PLUS status line, which appears at the foot of the screen. Scoreboard messages will instead appear on line 0 unless they are suppressed with SET SCOREBOARD OFF. Default of SET STATUS is ON.

● **SET STEP ON** is used to single step your way through a program. After each command, you will be asked if you want to do another step, i.e. execute another single command, or cancel the program. If SET ECHO ON has also been issued, each command will be displayed prior to the selection message. Default is OFF.

● **SET TALK OFF** is used in programs to prevent the display of dBASE messages such as the current record number. Default is ON.

● **SET TYPEAHEAD TO** sets the size of the typeahead buffer. See the CLEAR TYPEAHEAD command for further information. A buffer size of up to 32000 may be specified. If SET ESCAPE is OFF, the SET TYPEAHEAD command will not work. The default setting is a buffer size of 20 characters.

● **SET UNIQUE** is used with the INDEX command to control duplicate items in the field that is being indexed. When SET UNIQUE is ON duplicates will be ignored. If you subsequently recreate such an index file with the REINDEX command, the original UNIQUE status will be maintained. Default is OFF.

● **SET VIEW TO** is used to open a .VUE view file. View files may be created with the CREATE VIEW command, which is a full screen command, or the CREATE VIEW FROM ENVIRONMENT command. The latter will create a .VUE file containing details of the current working environment, i.e. the names of all open database files and associated indexes, selected work areas including relationships created by the SET RELATIONSHIP TO command, and so forth. On a subsequent occasion the entire working environment may be recreated in one command:

```
set view to filename
```

The SET VIEW TO command will read the specified .VUE file and use its contents to open database files, index files, and so forth. It will then close the .VUE file. The .VUE file may also be modified with MODIFY VIEW, a full screen operation which cannot be performed from within a program.

The SKIP command

Syntax: SKIP numeric expression

The SKIP command moves the current record pointer forwards or backwards in the database file currently in USE. If an index is active, the movement will be in the indexed sequence. Used on its own, SKIP will move forward one record. A movement of greater than one record may be specified by adding a numeric value to the command. If the numeric value is negative, the movement will be backwards towards the beginning of the file.

The RECNO( ) function may be used to obtain the current record number at any time, and the EOF( ) and BOF( ) functions may be used to test whether the record representing the end of file or beginning of file respectively has been reached.

The SORT command

Syntax: SORT TO filename ON key fields [sequence] [scope]
        [FOR/WHILE condition]

The SORT command creates a new database file in which the

records of the database currently in USE are resequenced according to the specified key field(s), for example:

```
sort to cars2 on make,model,cost
```

The TO clause provides the filename of the sorted file. The ON clause specifies the key field or fields which will control the sort sequence of the output file. The sorting operation will sort fields into ascending sequence unless a descending sequence is specified by adding /D to the fieldname, for example:

```
sort on cost/d to carscost
```

The same sequencing syntax may be used to specify that you do not want differences between upper and lower-case characters to be observed, by adding /C to the fieldname. The three sequencing clauses are:

/D for descending
/A for ascending (which is the default)
/C to ignore case differences

The /C clause may be used in combination with /A or /D as follows:

```
sort on make/dc to carsmake
```

As an alternative you may use the keywords DESCENDING or ASCENDING in place of /D and /A although this syntax is not available with the Clipper compiler. In the dBASE II specification the DESCENDING or ASCENDING keywords are the only means of specifying a sequence. The SCOPE and FOR/WHILE clauses are not available in the dBASE II specification, nor may you have more than one key field.

Note that in the dBASE III specification you may mix field types such as character, numeric, and date for a single sort operation. Logical or Memo fields may not be used in the ON clause, nor may functions or expressions. The SCOPE clause allows you to limit the command, for example by specifying the NEXT one or more records. The FOR/WHILE clauses allow you to impose conditions on the records to be processed in the course of the SORT command.

The STORE command

Syntax: STORE expression TO memory variable(s)
        memory variable = expression

The STORE command is used to move data from one memory variable to another, or from a database field to a memory variable. You cannot STORE a variable to a database field. The REPLACE command performs this function.

The STORE command also creates memory variables. In the dBASE language memory variables are not declared or defined before use. They come into being when they are used to receive the contents of a database field or the result of an expression, for example:

```
store make to makex
store 0 to lines,pages
tax = .3 * profit
```

None of the four variables shown in the example, MAKEX, LINES, PAGES, or TAX, needs to have existed earlier; they would be created by the lines shown above. If they had existed they would have been overwritten.

The STORE command also assigns the type characteristic to a variable in the sense that the created variable will be of the same type as the expression stored to it:

```
store 123   to var1
store "abc" to var2
store .T. to var3
store ctod("12/12/86") to var4
display memory
```

```
VAR1          pub  N          123
VAR2          pub  C   "abc"
VAR3          pub  L   .T.
VAR4          pub  D   12/12/86
```

Note that dBASE III and dBASE III PLUS do not allow you to STORE Memo fields, although Clipper does.

The fact that you can change the type of a variable means that you can create program bugs by using a careless STORE command, for example by storing a value when you meant to store a character string, only to find that a subsequent test fails to work.

If you use a memory variable that has the same name as a field in an active database, the field will take precedence over the variable unless you prefix the name with $m->$, for example:

```
store m->make to makex
```

The two syntaxes of the STORE command are interchangeable, but the assignment (=) syntax cannot be used when you want to store the same expression to more than one variable in a single command. The assignment syntax is not available in the dBASE II specification.

There is a fixed number of memory variables that may be created, although the different implementations of the dBASE language vary on this point. dBASE II allows a maximum of 64 variables, the FoxBASE equivalent 128, dBASE III 256, and Clipper several thousand.

The SUM command

Syntax: SUM [scope] field list TO memory variable list
        [FOR/WHILE condition]

This command provides a total for each of the specified fields for all records in the database file currently in USE or only for those records which meet the specified condition(s).

In the interpreters like dBASE II, FoxBASE, and dBASE III, the command may be used interactively, i.e. without supplying the names of memory variables which are to receive the result(s) of the command. In a dBASE program, the memory variables are necessary since without these you could not display the result(s).

The SCOPE clause allows you to limit the command, for example by specifying the NEXT one or more records. The FOR/WHILE clauses allow you to impose conditions on the records to be processed in the course of the SUM command. A typical use of the conditional clause would be as follows:

```
store "BMW" to makex
sum cost to costx for make = makex
? makex," : Total Cost of Vehicles = ",costx
```

By its nature, the SUM command implies that its usage is restricted to numeric fields only. An error will result if you try to specify a non-numeric field.

The SUSPEND command

Syntax: SUSPEND

This dBASE III PLUS command is used in debugging a program and is coupled with the RESUME command. SUSPEND stops the program and returns control to the dot prompt, where you can execute commands interactively until you want the program to continue execution. Then you issue the RESUME command and the program will carry on from the command line following the SUSPEND command. All current memory variables, including those which are not PUBLIC, will be intact during the period of suspension so that you are able to carry on using them, or examine them with the DISPLAY MEMORY command.

The TEXT command

Syntax: TEXT [TO PRINT] [TO FILE filename]
        lines of text
        ENDTEXT

The TEXT/ENDTEXT commands operate as a pair. Any lines of text contained between these two commands are displayed exactly as they appear. Delimiters are not required and macros appearing within the lines of text will not be expanded.

If the SET PRINT ON command has previously been issued, the lines of text will be directed to the printer. The Clipper compiler also supports output to a printer by means of adding the TO PRINT clause to the TEXT command, or output to a disk file by means of the TO FILE clause.

The TOTAL command

Syntax: TOTAL ON key field TO filename [scope]
        [FIELDS field list] [FOR/WHILE condition]

The TOTAL command may be used to summarise all or part of a database file. It is effectively a sub-totalling command, but it does so by creating a second database file containing one record for every sub-total. In order to sub-total successfully, the database file in USE must be indexed or sorted on the key field specified by the ON clause.

The SCOPE clause allows you to limit the command, for example by specifying the NEXT one or more records. The FOR/WHILE clauses allow you to impose conditions on the records to be processed in the course of the TOTAL command.

The new database file will contain all the fields of the original, but except for the numeric fields that contain the sub-totals, the other fields will contain the data from the first record in each group. The TOTAL command may be qualified with the FIELDS clause which specifies the field(s) to be sub-totalled. Numeric fields not included in the FIELDS clause will still be transferred to the new database file, but they will be treated as non-numeric fields, i.e. not sub-totalled and will therefore contain data from the first record in the group.

One aspect requires care when using the TOTAL command and that is the possibility of numeric overflow. Since the new database file will have a structure that is an exact duplicate of the original, it is possible that a sub-total of a numeric field will not fit because it contains more digits than the numeric field itself was designed to contain.

The TYPE Command

Syntax: TYPE filename [TO PRINT]

The TYPE command will display the contents of any text file. The filename extension must be provided, even if the file is a program file, for example:

```
type cars01.prg
```

Because the TYPE command opens the file that it is to display, you cannot use it on files that are already open. This means that you are unable to TYPE programs while they are executing.

If the SET PRINT ON command has been issued previously, output from the TYPE command will also be directed to the printer. In the dBASE III specification, the same effect may be obtained by adding the TO PRINT clause to the command.

The UPDATE command

dBASE II syntax:
   UPDATE FROM filename ON field [ADD field list]
      [REPLACE field list WITH field list] [RANDOM]
dBASE III syntax:
   UPDATE FROM alias ON field [REPLACE field WITH
      expression] [RANDOM]

This command allows you to use the information contained in one database file to change a second. The ON clause is used to specify a field which is used to achieve a match on the records from the two databases. Thus if the ON clause specified a surname field in both databases, the information contained in the JONES record of the FROM database could be used to update the information contained in the JONES record of the database file currently in USE. In the dBASE III specification, the FROM clause is used to specify an alias not a filename.

Before looking at the update procedure itself, let us first consider the method of achieving a match. Both databases must be in the same sequence, either sorted or indexed in the sequence specified by the key field of the ON clause. If RANDOM is specified, the database in USE must be indexed on the key field specified in the ON clause, but the FROM database may follow any sequence. In the dBASE II specification, if RANDOM is not specified, the FROM database must be sorted to the correct sequence, not indexed.

Once a match has taken place the fields in the FROM database will be used to update the fields contained in the database in USE. The REPLACE clause specifies which FROM fields are to update which fields of the database in USE.

In the dBASE III specification the FROM fields must be identified by the appropriate alias:

```
replace cost with b->newcost
```

Note, however, that the syntax specifies an expression for the FROM database not a field. This means that you can apply a calculation to the field of the database in USE, for example by adding to it the contents of the FROM field:

```
replace cost with cost + b->increase
```

In the dBASE II specification you are more limited but you can use the ADD clause in similar fashion to add the FROM field to that of the database file in USE. Note, however, that the ADD clause requires that both fieldnames are the same.

The USE command

Syntax: USE filename [INDEX file list] [ALIAS alias name]

The USE command opens a database file for use by other dBASE commands. The filename may be (and usually is) supplied without an extension, in which case a .DBF extension is assumed. On its own, the USE command will close the database file currently in USE as well as any related indexes that may be open at the time.

Up to seven indexes may be specified with the INDEX keyword, their filenames separated by commas. The first of these will dictate the sequence of the information held in the database file, but all the specified indexes will be updated if you change the database, for example if you add extra records or make changes to existing records. The SET ORDER TO command may be used to select a different controlling index.

As an alternative to specifying indexes within the USE command, you may do so with the SET INDEX TO command. Remember when doing so to specify *all* the indexes you require, since the SET INDEX TO command will close any that have been specified previously. For practical purposes you are advised to avoid specifying more than one index in dBASE II itself, since it is capable of taking over-long in updating the indexes when changes are made to the database file.

The USE command operates within the currently selected work area. In the dBASE II specification there are only two work areas: the primary and the secondary, and you may have a database file in USE within each of these. In the dBASE III specification you may have up to ten work areas with a database file in USE in each. The SELECT command transfers execution from one work area to another. In the dBASE III specification, the work areas are identified by the first ten letters of the alphabet or the numbers 1 to 10, but an alternative in the form of an ALIAS exists. This simply means that you are allowed to use a familiar or convenient name (known as an alias) instead of a letter of the alphabet to denote a given work area. The way that you specify your choice is by including such a name in the USE command following the keyword ALIAS:

```
select 2
use staff alias emp1
select 3
use empnames alias emp2
select emp1
```

Another consideration in the dBASE III specification is the existence of Memo fields with the corresponding use of .DBT files. Where Memo fields have been specified, the USE command will automatically open the associated .DBT file when it opens the database and index files. If the .DBT file has been deleted, the open will fail.

After a database file has been opened, the current record will be either the first physical record in the database file, i.e. record 1, or it will be the first logical record as per the sequence dictated by the first index file specified as part of the USE command.

The WAIT command

Syntax: WAIT [prompt] [TO variable]

This command displays a message on the screen and then suspends execution of the program until the user presses a key, before it allows the program to continue. In the dBASE II specification the message is 'Waiting', in the dBASE III specification it is 'Press any key to continue' unless you supply your own prompt. Remember to enclose your prompt in quotes or square brackets.

The prompt is not available in the dBASE II specification, but if you want to suppress the 'Waiting' message you do so by using the SET CONSOLE OFF command immediately before issuing the WAIT command, following the latter with SET CONSOLE ON. This technique is especially useful when using the WAIT TO form of the command which allows you to find out which key was pressed to end the waiting:

```
? "Enter P if report to be printed, any other key if not."
set console off        .
wait to reply
set console off
if reply = "p" .or. reply = "P"
   set print on
endif
```

In the dBASE III specification the above becomes unnecessary since you can supply your own prompt, even one containing a null variable if you want to suppress the 'Press any key to continue' message:

```
wait "" to reply
```

You should be careful too, in the dBASE III specification, to test the length of the memory variable which received the reply, since a null variable can be generated if the user presses the Return key only:

```
wait to reply
if .not. len(reply) = 0
  if reply = "p" .or. reply = "P"
     set print on
  endif
endif
```

The ZAP command

Syntax: ZAP

The ZAP command will delete all records from the database file currently in USE. It is equivalent to DELETE ALL followed by PACK, but much faster since it does not read through the database file in order to perform the operation. Instead it resets to zero a count in the database header which shows the number of records in the file. In addition, the ZAP command will reset to their minimum size all open index and .DBT memo files which are associated with the database.

Unless the SET SAFETY OFF command is in force, a caution will be displayed before the ZAP command starts work:

```
. zap
Zap C:cars.dbf? (Y/N)
```

Chapter Six
The dBASE Functions

This chapter examines dBASE functions in three ways: first by grouping them into functional categories, then listing them alphabetically and discussing each one individually, and finally looking at how you would go about creating and using your own functions.

In dBASE II there were only 16 functions. When dBASE III arrived, it brought 36 functions. The Clipper compiler again boosted the number of functions. It also added the means of creating your own functions. dBASE III PLUS brought yet another set of functions, some of which reflected those in the compiler. At the time of writing there are some 80 functions.

Functions which are not available in dBASE III versions earlier than dBASE III PLUS are indicated by a large dot in the summary of functions given below. Those which, at the time of writing, appear only in dBASE III PLUS are indicated by a P, while those which appear only with the Clipper compiler are indicated by a C. Bear in mind, however, that since the latest specification of the dBASE interpreter and its compilers will continually reflect one another, these distinctions may be rendered out of date by the appearance of new versions of the software products.

Although the dBASE II syntax will be shown separately in the short functional summary that follows, to avoid constant repetition only the dBASE III syntax will be used in the discussions of the functions. As a general point you should note that in dBASE III syntax all function keywords are followed by round brackets. Often these enclose data, such as SQRT(16) to find the square root of 16, but in the case of a number of functions such as EOF( ) the brackets are there to differentiate between a field or variable name and a dBASE III function.

Functional classification

dBASE II specification

1. Functions related to files and records:

#	: current record number (RECNO in dBASE III)
*	: deleted record indicator (DELETED in dBASE III)
EOF	: end of file indicator
FILE	: file existence indicator

2. Functions providing special tests:

@	: to find out whether and where a character string is contained in another character string (AT in dBASE III)
LEN	: to find out how many characters a character string contains
TYPE	: indicates the type, i.e. character, numeric, or logical, of a field or memory variable

3. Functions related to numeric or character variables:

!	: to convert lower-case characters to upper-case (UPPER in dBASE III)
$	: to obtain a character string which is part of another character string (SUBSTR in dBASE III)
CHR	: provides a character which represents a given numeric value
RANK	: provides the ASCII value that represents a given character (ASC in dBASE III)
STR	: to turn a numeric field into a character string
TRIM	: display or print a character string without allowing trailing blanks to take up space
VAL	: to turn a character string into a numeric field

4. Mathematical functions:

INT	: to discard the fraction and return only the integer value

5. Date and time functions:

DATE	: to obtain the system date

dBASE III specification

1. Functions related to files and records:

	BOF	: beginning of file indicator
●P	DBF	: name of database file currently in use
	DELETED	: deleted record indicator
●P	DISKSPACE	: number of bytes available on default drive
	EOF	: end of file indicator
●	FIELD	: to obtain the name of any field in a database file (also known as FIELDNAME)
	FILE	: file existence indicator
●	FOUND	: to test if a record search was successful
●	LASTREC	: to obtain a count of the number of records in a database file (Clipper only: see RECCOUNT)
●P	NDX	: name of specified active index file
●	RECCOUNT	: identical to LASTREC function, but RECCOUNT is valid in dBASE III PLUS and Clipper
	RECNO	: current record number
●P	RECSIZE	: size in bytes of record in currently selected database

2. Functions providing special tests:

	AT	: to find out whether and where a character string is contained in another character string
●C	EMPTY	: to find out whether an expression is empty of data
●	IF	: to provide conditional processing of expressions (Clipper only: see IIF)
●	IIF	: identical to IF function, but IIF is valid in dBASE III PLUS and Clipper
●	INKEY	: to obtain the ASCII value of any key that is pressed
●	ISALPHA	: to test if a letter is alphabetic
●P	ISCOLOR	: to test if the screen mode is colour or monochrome
●	ISLOWER	: to test if a character is lower-case
●	ISUPPER	: to test if a character is upper-case
●	LASTKEY	: to obtain the ASCII value of the key that has been pressed most recently (Clipper only: see READKEY)
●	LUPDATE	: to obtain the date when the currently selected database was last updated
●	LEN	: to find out how many characters a character

string contains.

- READKEY : to find out which key has been pressed to leave a full screen display, and whether changes have been made (dBASE III PLUS only: see LASTKEY)

  TYPE : indicates the type, i.e. character, numeric, logical, date, or memo of a field or memory variable

- ●C UPDATED : to find out whether the most recent READ command resulted in any changes to the associated GETS

3. Functions related to numeric, character or memo variables:

  ASC : provides the ASCII value that represents a given character (equates to the RANK function in dBASE II)

  CHR : provides a character which represents a given numeric value

- LEFT : to obtain the leftmost part of a character string

  LOWER : to convert upper-case characters to lower-case

- LTRIM : to remove leading spaces
- ●C MEMOEDIT : allows you to display or change the contents of Memo fields or variables
- REPLICATE : to repeat a character expression a specified number of times
- RIGHT : to obtain the rightmost part of a character string
- RTRIM : to remove trailing spaces (identical to TRIM)

  SPACE : to generate a fixed number of blank spaces

  STR : to turn a numeric field into a character string

- STUFF : to replace a part of a character string

  SUBSTR : to obtain a character string which is part of another character string

- TRANSFORM : to allow PICTURE formatting characters in commands such as LIST, DISPLAY, ? and REPORT

  TRIM : to remove trailing spaces

  UPPER : to convert lower-case characters to upper-case

  VAL : to turn a character string into a numeric field

- ●C WORD : used with the CALL command to convert numeric parameters from a data type of DOUBLE to a data type of INT to reduce the amount of data storage required by the called routine

4. Mathematical functions:

- ABS : to obtain the absolute value of a numeric expression

	EXP	: to return the value of e in e^x from x
	INT	: to discard the fraction and return only the integer value
	LOG	: to return the logarithm of a value
●	MAX	: to obtain the larger of two values
●	MIN	: to obtain the smaller of two values
●	MOD	: to obtain the remainder of a division
	ROUND	: to round a value with decimal places up or down to a smaller number of decimal places
	SQRT	: to calculate the square root of a given value

5. Date and time functions:

	CDOW	: to obtain the day of the week name from a dBASE III date field or variable
	CMONTH	: to obtain the month name from a dBASE III date field or variable
	CTOD	: to convert a character string containing a date to a dBASE III date variable
	DATE	: to obtain the system date
	DAY	: to obtain the day of the month from a dBASE III date field or variable
	DOW	: to obtain the day number in the week from a dBASE III date field or variable
	DTOC	: to convert a dBASE III date field or variable to a character string
●C	DTOS	: to convert a dBASE III date field or variable to a character string in the form YYYYMMDD
	MONTH	: to obtain the month number from a dBASE III date field or variable
●C	SECONDS	: to obtain the system time in seconds
	TIME	: to obtain the current time
	YEAR	: to obtain the year in the form 19XX from a dBASE III date field or variable

6. Functions related to screen and printer:

	COL	: returns the current screen column position of the cursor
	ROW	: returns the current screen row position of the cursor
	PCOL	: returns the current printer column position of the cursor
	PROW	: returns the current printer row position of the cursor

7. Functions that provide identification:

●P   ERROR   : to obtain the error message number resulting from the ON ERROR command

●P   GETENV   : to obtain parameters from the operating system environment

●P   FKLABEL   : to obtain the name of a requested function key

●P   FKMAX   : to determine the maximum number of function keys

●P   MESSAGE   : to obtain the error message resulting from the ON ERROR command

●P   OS   : to obtain the name and version of the operating system

●C   PROCLINE   : to obtain the source line number of the program or procedure currently being executed

●C   PROCNAME   : to obtain the name of the program or procedure currently being executed

●C   SELECT   : to obtain the number of the currently selected work area

●   VERSION   : to obtain the name and version of the dBASE software

Alphabetic list of functions

● The **ABS** function provides the absolute value of a numeric expression so that you can, for example, obtain the unsigned difference between two values:

```
. ? abs(7.55 - 9.333)
1.783
```

● The **ASC** function (RANK function in dBASE II) provides you with a means of obtaining the ASCII code value of a character. For example, ASC('A') will produce 65 while ASC('B') will produce 66. The name of a field may be supplied in place of the character itself, but only the leftmost character of the field will be evaluated.

● The **AT** function (@ in dBASE II) or substring search function searches a character field for a specified character or set of characters and returns a value that shows the starting position of the character(s) if found, or zero if it was not found. The syntax is:

AT(a,b)

where:

  a : character expression to be found
  b : character expression to be searched

Both expressions have to be character strings. Typically the first expression would be a user reply and the second a fieldname, for example if you want to examine records for a given surname and display those that match, surname first:

```
store at(reply,name) to start
if .not. start = 0
  ? trim(substr(name,start))+",",substr(name,1,len(trim(name))-start)
endif
skip
```

● The **BOF** function signals that you have reached the beginning of the file by returning a logical True condition.

● The **CDOW** or day of the week name function operates on a date variable or expression and returns a character string containing the day of the week:

```
. ? cdow(dat)
Saturday
```

● The **CHR** function is the opposite to ASC in that the function CHR will convert a numeric value to the equivalent character, for example CHR(65) will produce the character A. Any expression may be used to produce the numeric value, including a fieldname or variable which contains the numeric value. The CHR function is typically used to send special characters to the screen or printer. Thus CHR(15) is commonly sent to an Epson printer to set it for condensed print. Similarly, CHR(27) and CHR(26) may be used respectively to obtain left and right arrow symbols on the screen, for example as part of your help messages to the user.

● The **CMONTH** or month name function operates on a date variable or expression and returns a character string containing the name of the month:

```
. ? cmonth(dat)
December
```

● The **COL** function returns the current column position of the cursor as a numeric value. It can be used in the same way as the ?? command to provide relative screen addressing, for example:

```
@ lines,0 say trim(make)
@ lines,col()+1 say trim(model)
```

This function can also be used to tell you when the cursor has reached a certain screen position:

```
do while col() < 75
```

● The **CTOD** or character to date conversion function is used to create a date type variable from a character string. The character string to be converted by CTOD must be in the form determined by the SET DATE command. If this command has not been issued, the required format will be MM/DD/YY, for example:

```
store ctod('12/27/86') to dat
```

If the SET DATE BRITISH command has been issued previously, the required format would be DD/MM/YY.

● The **DATE** function is used to obtain the current date from the DOS date store. The result will be a date variable. The DATE function may itself be used with any of the date functions, for example:

```
. ? cdow(date())
Friday
```

● The **DAY** or day of the month function operates on a date variable or expression and returns a numeric value containing the day of the month:

```
. ? day(dat)
27
```

● The **DBF** function returns a character string containing the filename of the database file currently in USE:

```
. use fees
. ? dbf()
C:fees.dbf
```

● The **DELETED** function may be used to find out whether or not a record has been marked for deletion:

```
if deleted()
  skip
else
  ? user
  skip
endif
```

The DELETED function returns a logical True or False depending on whether or not the current record has been marked for deletion.

● The **DISKSPACE** function allows you to find out how much space is left on the disk which is currently being used in the default drive. DISKSPACE returns a numeric value giving the number of bytes available. You could, for example, use the function to test that there is enough space to create an index, or monitor the addition of new records to obtain an early warning of a disk full situation. The RECSIZE function is a useful companion in such tests, but remember to allow for simultaneous increases in your index files.

● The **DOW** or day of the week number function operates on a date variable or expression and returns a numeric value representing the day of the week:

```
. ? dow(dat)
7
```

● The **DTOC** function converts a date variable into a character string:

```
. store dtoc(dat) to chardate
27/12/86
```

```
. display memory
DAT          pub    D 27/12/86
CHAR         pub    C "27/12/86"
```

● The **DTOS** function operates on a date variable or field and returns a character string in the form YYYYMMDD, for example the date 28/12/86 will be returned as 19861228. DTOS is particularly useful when you want to index on a date field in combination with a character field:

```
index on supplier+dtos(invdate) to invoices
```

● The **EMPTY** function allows you to test for the following:

● a character string containing only spaces
● a null character string
● a numeric value of zero

● an empty date
● a logical False

EMPTY returns a logical True on any of the above. Be careful if you are using it to test for a null character variable that you do not overlook a variable containing a space.

● The **EOF** function returns a logical True when the end of the database file currently in USE has been reached. Note that when EOF is true in dBASE II, the current record number will be that of the last record, while in dBASE III it will be the last record plus one. This applies even if the file is being used with an index.

● The **ERROR** function may be used to obtain the error message number resulting from the ON ERROR command. It is similar in use to the MESSAGE function which returns the error message as opposed to the error number. The error number will be returned as a numeric data type.

● The **EXP** function is the opposite of the LOG function and has the syntax:

exp(numeric expression)

For example:

```
. ? exp(2.08)
      8.00
```

● The **FIELD** or **FIELDNAME** function operates on the database file currently in USE and returns a character string containing the name of a requested field number. The fieldname will be returned as an upper-case character string. For example, to find out the fieldname of the second field of the database:

```
. ? field(2)
YEAR
```

If the specified field number is greater than the number of fields in the database, a null string will be returned. The FIELD function allows you to process database fields as an array, for example to list names and address lines without including unused address lines:

```
use names
set talk off
do while .not. eof()
   fieldno = 1
   do while fieldno < 7
     fname = field(fieldno)
     if &fname = ' '
       exit
     endif
     ? &fname
     fieldno = fieldno + 1
   enddo
   skip
enddo
```

If you want to know how many fields there are in a database, for example if you want to calculate the size of your database file header (see under the RECSIZE function), you can perform a loop until a null string is returned:

```
fno = 0
null = ""
do while null < field(fno+1)
   fno = fno + 1
enddo
? "Number of fields =",fno
```

● The **FILE** function is used to test for the existence of a file and returns a logical True if the file was found:

```
store "names" to fname
 if file(fname+".dbf")
  use &fname
 else
```

● The **FKLABEL** function tells you the name of a requested function key that may be programmed. FKLABEL returns a character string:

```
. ? fklabel(1)
F2
```

```
. ? fklabel(9)
F10
```

The examples above are from an IBM PC where F1 is the HELP key, hence Function key 2 is the first key that can be reprogrammed with the SET FUNCTION command.

● The **FKMAX** function returns an integer that gives the highest number of programmable function keys. The example below is again taken from an IBM PC:

```
. ? fkmax()
9
```

● The **FOUND** function returns a logical True or False to indicate whether the previous FIND, SEEK, LOCATE or CONTINUE command was successful.

```
. find 90525
. ? found()
.T.
. find 50525
No find.
. ? found()
.F.
```

The FOUND function can be used as an alternative to the EOF( ) test on index lookup operations. Note that the condition returned by the FOUND function tells you whether the current record number represents the record you were looking for. If, therefore, you change the current record number with a command such as SKIP or GO, the FOUND condition will be reset to False.

● The **GETENV** or Get Environment function returns a character string which contains the setting of a requested named parameter in the operating system environment. For example, the SET command in DOS allows you to store parameters in a special area of memory which is accessible by all programs. Let us suppose that you had inserted the Chinese year into the environment by issuing the DOS command as follows:

```
SET year=RAT
```

In dBASE, you could access this with a STORE command:

```
. store getenv('year') to chinyear
. ? chinyear
RAT
```

The name of the parameter, i.e. 'YEAR' in the example, may be given in upper or lower-case but must be enclosed in quotes.

● The **IF** or **IIF** function enables you to perform conditional processing within a single command line. What happens is that you ask the function to evaluate a condition, for example one that tests the sex of a parent in order to include the word 'mother' or 'father' in a personalised letter. Then you supply two more expressions. If the condition is True, the first expression will be returned. If it is False, the second will be returned:

```
parent = if(sex = "F", "mother", "father")
```

The syntax is thus:

if(a,b,c)

where:

   a : conditional expression
   b : expression to be returned if condition is true
   c : expression to be returned if condition is false

The expressions to be returned may have a type of character, numeric or date provided both are of the same type. As you can see, the function cannot provide more than two alternatives but it is nevertheless very useful in any logical situation where a yes/no condition applies.

● The **INKEY** function returns the ASCII numeric value of the next key to be pressed. It will also return a value of zero if no key is pressed. By employing the INKEY function as part of a loop that is producing a long report or a long display you are able to give users a means of interrupting the sequence. As soon as INKEY( ) returns a value other than zero you know that the user is trying to attract attention. Used as INKEY( ), the INKEY function does not resemble the ACCEPT command in waiting for a key depression: it is simply a means of testing whether a key has been pressed. You have to be careful, however, in interpreting this, since with the keyboard buffer a keyed value could have been sitting there for some time, waiting for attention. There is also an alternative syntax which does create a pause:

INKEY(0)   will halt the execution of the program until a key is pressed

INKEY(expression) where the expression is larger than zero, will wait that number of seconds for a key to be pressed before continuing execution of the program.

Other than being able to tell that the user wants attention, the INKEY function does, of course, allow you to tell which key has been pressed. This is particularly useful in an application that wants to make use of control keys such as the arrow keys or the Return key or Insert and **Delete** keys. The following gives the ASCII values for some of these keys:

Right arrow	or CNTRL and D	4
Left arrow	or CNTRL and S	19
Cursor up	or CNTRL and E	5
Cursor down	or CNTRL and X	24
Insert	or CNTRL and V	22
Delete	or CNTRL and G	7
Home	or CNTRL and A	1
End	or CNTRL and F	6
PgUp	or CNTRL and R	18
PgDn	or CNTRL and C	3
RETURN		13
ESCAPE		27

● The integer function **INT** provides a means of discarding the decimal part of a value, i.e. the fraction, to return the integer or whole number. The syntax is:

int(numeric expression)

The whole number will retain its sign, so that it will remain negative if the value was negative to start with. You may round up by adding .5 to the value within the expression, for example:

```
. store 19.6 to cost
. ? int(cost+0.5)
        20
```

● The **ISALPHA** function examines a character string and returns a logical True if the first character of the string is alphabetic, either upper or lower-case.

```
. ? isalpha('1')
.F.
. ? isalpha('A4567')
.T.
. ? isalpha('ə')
.F.
```

● The **ISCOLOR** function allows you to test whether dBASE is running in monochrome or colour mode. It returns a logical True for colour, logical False for monochrome.

```
. ? iscolor()
.F.
```

The function is used in association with the SET COLOR TO command. Note that the SET COLOR OFF command can set the screen to monochrome mode even if you are using a colour monitor.

● The **ISLOWER** function examines a character string and returns a logical True if the first character of the string is lower-case alphabetic.

```
. ? islower('1')
.F.
. ? islower('a')
.T.
. ? islower('Abcdef')
.F.
```

● The **ISUPPER** function examines a character string and returns a logical True if the first character of the string is upper case alphabetic.

```
. ? isupper('1')
.F.
. ? isupper('aBCDE')
.F.
. ? isupper('ABCdef')
.T.
```

● The **LASTKEY** gives you the ASCII numeric value of the last key pressed. This allows you to test for the use of keys such as the Escape key:

```
if lastkey() = 27
   exit
endif
```

● The **LASTREC** or **RECCOUNT** function provides you with a numeric value giving the record number of the last record in the database file currently in USE. This, of course, is also a count of the number of records in the database. The syntax is:

LASTREC( )

● The **LEFT** function is similar in operation to the SUBSTR function in that it extracts part of a character string, except that it always begins at the leftmost character of the string. The syntax is:

LEFT(a,b)

where:

a : character expression which may be a fieldname or variable name
b : number of characters

If you ask for too many characters relative to the length of the string, you will get the whole string.

● The **LEN** function provides a numeric value giving the length of a character string. Note, however, that trailing spaces are also considered to be characters. If you want to ignore trailing spaces, you should include the TRIM function, e.g.:

```
? len("123456     ")
      11

? len(trim("123456     "))
      6
```

● The **LOG** function returns the the logarithm of a value and has the following syntax:

log(numeric expression)

For example:

```
. ? log(8)
     2.08
```

● The **LOWER** function converts upper-case characters to lower-case. It is the opposite of the UPPER function but otherwise it performs in exactly the same way.

● The **LTRIM** function removes leading spaces from a character string in contrast to TRIM which removes trailing spaces. LTRIM is especially useful for removing the spaces which result from the use of the STR function. An example of the use of LTRIM is given under the RIGHT function.

● The **LUPDATE** function returns a date that shows when the database currently in USE was last updated. The result will have a date data type that may be used with other date functions, for example subtracted from the result of the system date function to find out how many days have elapsed since the file was last updated.

```
. store lupdate() to previous
. ? previous
01/24/86
. ? type('previous')
D
. set date british
. ? previous
24/01/86
. ? date() - previous
        12
```

● The **MAX** function returns the value resulting from the higher of two numeric expressions. The syntax is:

max(numeric expression,numeric expression)

The function is useful within DO loops, for example:

```
do while max(field1,field2) > 1000
```

● The **MEMOEDIT** function comes with the Clipper compiler and allows you to display or change the contents of Memo fields or variables. It also allows you to set up a screen window within which the Memo will appear. The syntax is as follows:

a = MEMOEDIT(b,c,d,e,f,g)

where:

  a : name of the Memo field or variable where the new Memo is to be stored. If you want to display the Memo only, this may be a null.
  b : name of the Memo field or variable that is to be displayed or changed.
  c : a numeric expression giving the row number of the top left corner of the screen to be used in displaying the Memo.
  d : a numeric expression giving the column number of the top left corner of the screen to be used in displaying the Memo.
  e : a numeric expression giving the row number of the bottom right corner of the screen to be used in displaying the Memo.
  f : a numeric expression giving the column number of the bottom right corner of the screen to be used in displaying the Memo.
  g : a logical expression which acts as an update indicator. If the Memo is to be updated, the expression should be set to True. If you simply want a display, it is set to False.

In the example below, the Memo field NOTES is being displayed:

```
If "" = Memoedit( Notes,6,11,14,59,.F.)
Endif [ Display Memo ]
```

In the example below the Memo field NOTES is being updated after the user has made changes to the Memo field:

```
Replace Notes With Memoedit( Notes,6,11,14,59,.T.)
```

The program module below is an example of a complete routine for displaying and updating Memo fields in a database called NAMES. It also demonstrates the use of the MENU TO command:

```
If .NOT. File ( 'c:\db311\names.Dbf' )
  ?
  ? ' Error Datafile "c:\db311\names.Dbf" not found.'
  ?
Endif [ Test For Datafile ]
*
use c:\db311\names
*
Clear
*
Bchars1 = Chr(201)+Chr(205)+Chr(187)+Chr(186)
Bchars2 = Chr(188)+Chr(205)+Chr(200)+Chr(186)
Bchars  = Bchars1+Bchars2
*
a 3,5 Say 'Name '
a 5,10,15,60 Box Bchars
a 20,0 Say Replicate('-',80)
a 22,0 Say Replicate('-',80)
*
Do While .T.
  Set Color To /w,w/
  a 3,15 Say Name
  Set Color To w+/,/w
  *
  If "" = Memoedit( Notes,6,11,14,59,.F.)
  Endif [ Display Memo ]
  *
  Set Message To 23
  a 21,11 Prompt ' Next '       Message ':- Display Next Record.'
  a 21,24 Prompt ' Previous '    Message ':- Display Previous Record.'
  a 21,40 Prompt ' Edit Memo '   Message ':- Edit The Text in The Box.'
  a 21,57 Prompt ' Quit '        Message ':- Leave Example Program.'
  Menu To Menu1
  *
```

```
Do Case
  Case (Menu1 = 0)  .OR. (Menu1 = 4)
    Close Data
    Quit
    *
  Case Menu1 = 1
    Skip
    If Eof()
      @ 23,0
      @ 23,10 Say 'This is the last record.  Press ANYKEY '
      Do ANYKEY
      Skip -1
    Endif [ Last Record Trap ]
    *
  Case Menu1 = 2
    Skip -1
    If Bof()
        @ 23,0
        @ 23,10 Say 'This is the First record.  Press ANYKEY '
        Do ANYKEY
      Endif [ Last Record Trap ]
      *
    Case Menu1 = 3
      Set Function 10 To Chr(23)
      @ 23,0
      @ 23,10 Say 'Press <F10> To Finish Edit .... '
      *
      Replace Notes With Memoedit( Notes,6,11,14,59,.T.)
  EndCase [ Do Menu Options ]
Enddo [ Cont. Loop ]
*
*
Procedure ANYKEY
  Do While Inkey() = 0
  Enddo [ Wait For Key ]
Return
```

● The **MESSAGE** function may be used to obtain the error message resulting from the ON ERROR command. It is similar in use to the ERROR function which returns the error number as opposed to the error message. The error message will be a character string which may be stored in a variable or displayed.

● The **MIN** function returns the value resulting from the lower of two numeric expressions. The syntax is:

min(numeric expression,numeric expression)

The function is useful if you want to test either of a pair of fields or variables whichever is the lower, for example within an IF statement:

```
if min(field1,field2) < 1000
```

● The **MOD** function returns the remainder of a division. The syntax is:

mod(numeric expression,numeric expression)

where the first expression is divided by the second.

```
. ? mod(145,12)
   1
```

The result will be signed according to the sign of the second expression.

● The **MONTH** or month number function operates on a date variable or expression and returns a numeric value containing the month number:

```
. ? month(dat)
12
```

● The **NDX** function returns the filename of a requested active index file:

```
. ? ndx(1)
C:fees.ndx
```

The result will be a character string. If there is no active index file in the requested position, a null string will be returned.

● The **OS** function returns a character string containing the name of the operating system currently in use:

```
. ? os()
DOS 2.10
```

● The **PCOL** function returns a numeric value giving the current column position of the printer. It can be used in the same way as the COL function to provide relative printer column addressing, or it can be used to tell you when the printer head has reached a certain column position on the page:

```
do while pcol() < 130
```

● The **PROCNAME** and **PROCLINE** functions may be used to return respectively the name and line number of the program or procedure in which the function is executed. The program name will be that of the original .PRG file and the line number will be that which contains the function, for example:

```
? procname(),procline()
CARS12       4
```

● The **PROW** function returns a numeric value giving the current row position of the printer. It can be used to provide relative printer line addressing, in the same way as the ROW function does on the screen. It can also be used to tell you when the printer has reached a certain line position, for example to tell you whether there is room enough to start a new heading:

```
if prow() > 50
  eject
```

● The **READKEY** function returns an integer that represents the key that was pressed in order to exit from one of the following full screen commands:

APPEND
BROWSE
CHANGE
CREATE
EDIT
INSERT
MODIFY
READ

Note that these are *not* the ASCII values of the keys such as the INKEY function would return. For example, INKEY would return a value of 3 for PgDn or CTRL and C, whereas READKEY returns 7 for the same key. Secondly, READKEY may give you one of two values for the same key depending on whether any changes have been made during the full screen operation. Thus a value of 7 indicates that the user left a screen (such as that presented by the EDIT command) with the PgDn key without making any changes, while a value of 263 (or 256 plus 7) indicates that the user left the screen with the PgDn key having made changes. Some of these keys with their values are shown below. The first value is returned if no data has been changed, the second value (an increment of 256) if the data has been changed.

Right arrow	or CNTRL and D	1 or 257
Left arrow	or CNTRL and S	0 or 256
Cursor up	or CNTRL and E	4 or 260
Cursor down	or CNTRL and X	5 or 261
Home	or CNTRL and A	2 or 258
End	or CNTRL and F	3 or 259
PgUp	or CNTRL and R	6 or 262
PgDn	or CNTRL and C	7 or 263
RETURN		16 or 272
ESCAPE		12 or 268

● The **RECCOUNT** function : see LASTREC function.

● The **RECNO** function returns a numeric value giving the current record number and may be used in commands such as STORE and GO, for example if you want to close and reopen the file without losing your place in the file:

```
store recno() to currec
use motor
go currec
```

There are one or two minor implementation differences that are worth noting. In dBASE II, you can reach record zero by using the SKIP command to go backwards. You cannot pass the last record by using the SKIP commands to go forwards if the last record is recorded as such in the .DBF header information, i.e. if the file has been closed properly. In dBASE III, if BOF( ) is true the current record number will be 1 but if EOF( ) is true, the current record number will be that of the last record plus one.

● The **RECSIZE** function returns a numeric value giving the size of the record in the database currently in USE. If you want to test whether there is enough room on a diskette to create a security copy of your database, you could multiply the results of the RECCOUNT and RECSIZE functions to obtain the size of the file in rough terms and compare this against the amount of space left on a diskette as given by the DISKSPACE function. If you want to obtain the precise size of the database file you would have to add the header size, which is calculated by taking 35 bytes and adding 32 bytes for each field. The number of fields can be obtained by using the FIELD function (see above).

● The **REPLICATE** function has the following syntax:

replicate(a,b)

where:

a : character expression
b : numeric expression

The numeric expression tells REPLICATE how many times to repeat the character expression. This function is very useful in @ SAY commands if you want to display or print special characters:

```
@ 12,0 say replicate(chr(205),80)
```

The above will draw a double-line border across the screen. Without the REPLICATE command this would be a very laborious procedure. (See also the @ BOX and @ TO commands.)

● The **RIGHT** function is similar in operation to the SUBSTR function in that it extracts part of a character string, except that it always begins at the rightmost character of the string and works backwards:

```
. store "abcdef" to chars
. ? right(chars,3)
def
```

The syntax is:

RIGHT(a,b)

where:

a : character expression which may be a fieldname or variable name
b : number of characters

If you ask for too many characters relative to the length of the string, you will get the whole string. An example of the use of the RIGHT function is in the printing of cheques. To print amounts in the form ****342.95 or **10342.95, you could do the following:

```
? right('**********'+ltrim(str(amount,10,2)),10)
```

The LTRIM function will trim any leading spaces resulting from the STR function and the RIGHT function will see to it that only the requisite number of asterisks is included to pad out the string to the maximum of 10 characters.

● The **ROUND** function is used to round a value with decimal places up or down to a smaller number of decimal places. The syntax is:

round(a,b)

where:

a : numeric expression to be rounded
b : numeric expression giving the number of decimal places required in the result

Let us look at an example:

```
. ? round(34.567,2)
34.570

. ? round(34.564,2)
34.560
```

If you want to round to tens or hundreds you would specify a negative number of decimal places so that −1 rounds to tens, −2 to hundreds, and so forth.

● The **ROW** function returns a numeric value giving the current row position of the cursor. It can be used to provide relative screen addressing in the same way as the COL function, or if you are formatting the screen to a specific design it can be used to tell you when the cursor has reached a certain screen position:

```
do while row() < 15
```

● The **RTRIM** function removes trailing spaces from a character string and is identical to the TRIM function.

● The **SECONDS** function returns the system time in seconds to 2 decimals. The value returned is the number of seconds that have elapsed since midnight. The range is 0 to 86399. SECONDS allow you to conduct timing exercises, for example on the length of time an indexing operation took, without having to convert the hours and minutes returned by the TIME function.

● The **SELECT** function returns a numeric value which gives the number of the currently selected work area.

● The **SPACE** function generates a fixed number of blank spaces:

```
store space(24) to surnamex
@ 10,0 say "Please enter surname " get surnamex
```

In dBASE II, which does not have this function, you can achieve the same result by using the STR function to convert a single digit to character form but specifying a large length for the resulting variable:

```
store str(1,25) to spaces
store $(spaces,1,24) to surnamex
```

The variable spaces will consist of 24 space characters followed by the character '1'. It is a simple matter to extract the first 24 characters using the substring function. If you do use this technique and then afterwards convert the program to dBASE III by means of the dCONVERT utility, you will find that dCONVERT does not understand what you have done. It takes a literal reading and simply converts the $ sign to SUBSTR, leaving the rest as it is. Unfortunately, the STR function in dBASE III gives an error if you specify an invalid length. You will, therefore, have to find each example and correct it by hand, using the SPACE function instead.

● The **SQRT** function calculates the square root of a given positive value. The syntax is:

sqrt(numeric expression)

The number of decimal places in the result will be equal to whichever is larger of that contained in the expression or that set as the dBASE default. The latter begins as 2 but may be changed by the SET DECIMAL command. The following examples show the difference:

```
. ? sqrt(4)
2.00

. store 55.6457 to num
. ? sqrt(num)
7.4596
```

● The **STR** function will convert a numeric value to character format and has the following syntax:

STR(a,b,c)

where:

a : numeric expression which may be a fieldname or variable name b : length of resulting character field

    c : number of decimals to be included

The length must provide a field long enough to contain all the significant digits (i.e. all those other than leading zeros) as well as the decimal point if decimals are required, and a minus sign if the value is negative. The STR function will round the decimals up or down to the nearest integer if you do not specify decimals. If you do not specify a length it will be set to ten characters by default, and with the Clipper compiler you will also get the default number of decimals. If STR is operating on a database field, this default will be the defined number of decimals for the field. In dBASE II you will get a syntax error if you do not specify the length.

● The **STUFF** function allows you to change part of a character string. You specify the start position and number of characters to be changed and then supply a new string which is to replace those characters. Remember that STUFF returns a character string containing the changes but it does not affect the original string. The syntax is:

    STUFF(a,b,c,d)

where:

    a : the string you want to change

    b : the start position

    c : the number of characters to be removed

    d : the replacement string

The replacement string does not have to be the same size as the number of characters being removed. In fact, if you simply want to remove certain characters you could do so by specifying a null string as the replacement.

● The **SUBSTR** function ($ in dBASE II) extracts part of a character field according to the following syntax:

    SUBSTR(a,b,c)

where:

    a : character expression which may be a fieldname or variable name

    b : start position

    c : number of characters

You do not have to specify the number of characters if you want to extract the whole of the rest of the string starting at the 'start position', for example:

```
. ? substr("123456789",5)
56789
```

Similarly, if you ask for too many characters relative to the length of the string, you will only get as many as are available in the string starting at the 'start position'.

● The **TIME** function is used to obtain the current time from the DOS time store. The result will be a character string in the form HH:MM:SS:

```
. ? time()
21:06:24
```

The TIME function may be used in time of day comparisons, for example:

```
if time() < "12"
   store "am" to timehdg
```

● The **TRANSFORM** function allows you to apply PICTURE formatting characters to fields in the following commands:

?
??
DISPLAY
LABEL
LIST
REPORT

The TRANSFORM function is used just as you would the UPPER or SUBSTR functions, for example:

```
list transform(cost,'99,999.99')
```

The only difference is that one of the parameters specifies the picture. All the PICTURE formatting characters including the @ sign function codes may be used. Let us look at a very simple example:

```
accept "Enter Name : " to namex
? transform(namex,'!!!!!!!')
return
```

This will produce the following on the screen:

```
Enter Name : fred
FRED
```

● The **TRIM** function removes trailing spaces in a character field. It is most useful when printing or displaying data, for example:

```
. display inits,name off
H.P.      Sorce

. display trim(inits)," ",name off
H.P. Sorce
```

● The **TYPE** function evaluates an expression (which could be a field or memory variable name) and tells you what data type it is by returning a single upper-case character : C for Character, N for Numeric, L for Logical, D for Date, M for Memo, or A for Array:

```
. store .T. to ind
.T.
. ? type('ind')
L
```

Note that if you are using a variable or fieldname it has to be enclosed in quote marks. However, you do not need quote marks if you have placed the name of a variable or field in another variable and the TYPE function is then evaluating the *contents* of a variable:

```
. store 99 to number
. store 'number' to field
. ? type(field)
N
```

If you use a variable or fieldname that does not exist, the response will be U for Undefined. Another purpose of the TYPE function is to evaluate whether an expression is valid or not:

```
. store 99 to number
. store "Jones" to name
. ? type('number*name')
U
```

Since you cannot multiply 99 by 'Jones', a U is returned.

● The **UPDATED** function returns a logical True if the most recent READ command resulted in any changes to the associated GETS. It enables you, for example, to perform REPLACE operations only if data items have been changed.

● The **UPPER** function (! in dBASE II) converts lower-case characters to upper-case. It is useful when you want to search for an item regardless of case and may be used to create an index which will reflect strict alphabetic sequence even when some items begin with a lower-case character.

● The **VAL** function is the converse of STR in that it converts a character field which contains leading numerics (including a decimal point and its sign if required) to a numeric value. Only the integer part of the value in the character field will be transferred to the numeric field. The syntax is:

VAL(character expression)

The expression may be the name of a field or variable and or even another function such as the substring function.

● The **VERSION** function returns a character string containing the software version number:

```
. ? version()
dBASE III PLUS  version 1.0
```

● The **WORD** function is used with the CALL command to convert numeric parameters from a data type of DOUBLE to a data type of INT to reduce the amount of data storage required by the called routine. An INT data type can hold a value of up to plus or minus 32K, so in many cases there is no need to pass a larger parameter such as a DOUBLE data type. However, if there is any possibility that the value to be passed may be beyond this range you should not use the WORD function. The syntax of the function is as follows:

CALL module name WITH WORD(numeric expression)

● The **YEAR** function operates on a date variable or expression and returns a numeric value containing the year in full form:

```
. ? year(dat)
1986
```

The YEAR function, in combination with the DAY and CMONTH

functions, is very useful for displaying a letter-style date such as 27 December 1986.

Creating your own functions

This section applies only to the Clipper compiler which (as described in Chapter 4) allows you to incorporate external routines at link time. Just to recap slightly, when confronted by a strange piece of syntax on a program line, such as FRED(54,23), the compiler does not automatically register an error but assumes that the strange syntax represents an external routine that will be made available at link time. Moreover, the compiler and the linker between them will manage to view the strange syntax according to dBASE rules. Thus, the presence of open and close round brackets will indicate that the strange syntax is a function, meaning that the brackets contain parameters which are to be passed on.

Now let us imagine that you have written a routine called FRED which expects two parameters and which returns a single parameter, and that you then compiled this routine and placed its object code in a library that would be included in the link process. Upon linking the main dBASE program, the link program would read this library file and extract from it your FRED routine. It would also ensure that your FRED routine received the two parameters contained in the FRED syntax and thereafter that the dBASE program received the single parameter returned by FRED.

Let us next look at what your FRED routine might look like:

```
FUNCTION FRED
*
* Syntax : FRED(a,b)
          where :
                    a : numeric expression 1
                    b : numeric expression 2
* Returns : The greater of two numbers
*
PARAMETERS num1, num2
RETURN IF(num1 > num2, num1, num2)
```

The FRED routine begins by using the FUNCTION command to declare the routine as a function and to give it its name. Then it uses the PARAMETERS command to receive the two expressions being passed to it. Next it uses the conditional IF function to test which of the two numbers is the larger and returns it. Since the IF function is part of the

RETURN command, this number is also returned to the calling module, i.e. to the dBASE program that contained the FRED syntax. And, suddenly, instead of FRED being a strange piece of syntax, it becomes a very useful function that compares two values and returns the greater. Indeed, if we had used the word MAX instead of the word FRED, we would have been discussing a perfectly valid dBASE function. Let us look at a few of these:

```
FUNCTION MIN
*
* Syntax : MIN(a,b)
*          where :
                    a : numeric expression 1
                    b : numeric expression 2
* Returns : The smaller of two numbers
*
PARAMETERS num1, num2
RETURN IF(num1 < num2, num1, num2)


FUNCTION RIGHT
*
* Syntax : RIGHT(a,b)
          where :
                    a : character expression
                    b : numeric expression
*
* Returns : The rightmost b characters of character expression a
*
PARAMETERS charstr, charlen
RETURN SUBSTR(charstr, LEN(charstr)-charlen+1)


FUNCTION STUFF
*
* Syntax : STUFF(a,b,c,d)
          where :
                    a : character expression 1
                    b : numeric expression 1
                    c : numeric expression 2
                    d : character expression 2
*
* Returns : Character expression 1 containing character
            expression 2 in place of the original characters
            starting at b with length c.
*
PARAMETERS charstr, charstart, charlen, charstr2
RETURN SUBSTR(charstr,1,charstart-1) + charstr2 + SUBSTR(charstr,charstart+charlen)
```

You will notice that all of these functions have been written in dBASE language, yet they represent functions which were not available in dBASE III until the advent of dBASE III PLUS. You could, of course, go further and write more complex functions in Assembler language or C, for example to count the number of .DBF files on a diskette. As a caution, however, before going ahead with your own routines you should examine the READ_ME file accompanying the Clipper compiler. You may find that the routine has already been provided.

Chapter Seven
Multi-User dBASE

At the time of writing there are only two multi-user dBASE software products on the market: FoxBASE from Fox Software and a special version of dBASE III PLUS. The former operates under Unix and Xenix, or on a local area network using network software such as that by Novell. The multi-user version of dBASE III PLUS (which is included as part of the single-user package) runs only on a local area network. As mentioned in Chapter 1, other multi-user editions of the dBASE language are on their way but until they arrive we can do no more than look at those already available.

dBASE III PLUS

The use of dBASE III PLUS in a multi-user environment relies on a local area network or LAN such as the Novell network. The multi-user version of dBASE III PLUS consists of three products:

- dBASE ADMINISTRATOR which is really just another version of dBASE III PLUS containing extra features for use with a network
- dBASE ACCESS which is loaded at each PC that requires access to dBASE ADMINISTRATOR
- PROTECT, a utility program that is used outside the dBASE environment to establish user log-in procedures, user access levels, and so forth

dBASE ADMINISTRATOR is installed on the network file server, and dBASE ACCESS on each PC workstation. dBASE ADMINISTRATOR and one copy of dBASE ACCESS is supplied as part of the dBASE III PLUS package; extra copies of dBASE ACCESS are available separately. To start up dBASE ADMINISTRATOR from a workstation the user would load the local ACCESS program, at the same time specifying the drive and directory which contains the dBASE

ADMINISTRATOR program. There is thus a single copy of the dBASE interpreter which resides on the file server and which may be used simultaneously by all users on the network, provided each has a unique copy of dBASE ACCESS.

Before we look at the special multi-user commands and functions which are available in dBASE ADMINISTRATOR, let us first consider what automatic features it provides. Commands which operate on an entire database file, for example COUNT or SORT, cannot be used unless the file is locked for the duration of the command. For this reason dBASE ADMINISTRATOR will automatically apply a file lock on the currently active database file before executing the command and then release the lock when execution of the command has been completed. This applies to the following commands:

APPEND BLANK	COPY STRUCTURE	REPLACE ALL
APPEND FROM	COUNT	SORT
AVERAGE	DELETE ALL	SUM
BROWSE	INDEX	TOTAL
CATALOG	JOIN	UPDATE
COPY	RECALL ALL	

dBASE ADMINISTRATOR opens files either for shared use or exclusive use. With the exception of databases and indexes, files that are written to are opened exclusively, while files that are used for read only purposes are opened for shared use. The list below illustrates this by showing the effect of the various file opening commands:

Exclusive use: COPY STRUCTURE (the TO file)
COPY (the TO file)
CREATE
CREATE/MODIFY LABEL
CREATE/MODIFY QUERY
CREATE/MODIFY REPORT
CREATE/MODIFY VIEW
INDEX (the TO file)
JOIN (the TO file)
MODIFY COMMAND
SAVE
SET ALTERNATE TO
SET INDEX TO
SORT (the TO file)
TOTAL (the TO file)

Shared use:

                          APPEND FROM (the FROM file)

                          DO

                          LABEL FORM

                          REPORT FORM

                          RESTORE

                          SET CATALOG TO

                          SET FORMAT TO

                          SET PROCEDURE TO

                          SET VIEW TO

                          UPDATE (the FROM file)

The files specified in the USE command, i.e. the database, index, and Memo files, may be opened in either mode according to the status specified by the SET EXCLUSIVE command. The default setting for the latter is SET EXCLUSIVE ON, which means that the USE command will normally open files for exclusive use unless you have issued the SET EXCLUSIVE OFF command. The clause EXCLUS-IVE may also be specified as part of the USE command if you want a specific database file to be exclusive while others are opened as shared, i.e. while SET EXCLUSIVE is OFF. Certain commands will result in an error message if the appropriate database files have not been opened exclusively. These are:

INSERT
MODIFY STRUCTURE
PACK
REINDEX
ZAP

Having examined the automatic multi-user features of dBASE ADMINISTRATOR, let us next turn to the commands and functions that allow us to control shared access to a particular database or its records. As will be obvious from the above, we have to start by opening the database file and its indexes for shared use:

```
set exclusive off
use names index names
set exclusive on
```

All users can thus have shared access to the NAMES database. However, we still have to prevent other users from trying to access a record at the same time as we are changing it. The commands we need to protect are REPLACE, and @ GET followed by a READ. Although the latter may just relate to a memory variable it could also change a database field if the field was used directly for the @ GET.

Since either REPLACE or READ would operate only on the current record, we need to lock just the one record. This is done by means of the LOCK( ) or RLOCK( ) function; the two are identical. The reason for having a function here rather than a command is that you get a two-in-one operation: it will carry out a test and perform an action. It tests the status of the current record and returns a logical False if it is already locked. You would then have to wait and try again as in the example below. If, however, the current record is not already locked, the function will lock it and then return a logical True condition. When you have changed its contents, you can unlock the record by means of the UNLOCK command. Let us look at an example:

```
do while .t.
  delay = 1
  do while .not. lock() .and. delay < 300
    delay = delay + 1
  enddo
  if delay # 300
    replace cost with costx, units with unitsx
    unlock
    exit
  else
    do telluser
    loop
  endif
enddo
```

Be careful not to repeat the use of the LOCK( ) function in a second test on the same record. The second time you will get a logical False since you will just have locked the record yourself.

A similar function is FLOCK( ) which attempts to lock the currently selected database file. If it is successful it returns a logical True, otherwise a logical False. A file so locked will remain locked until it is unlocked by means of the UNLOCK command, or it is closed, or the user leaves dBASE. The UNLOCK command may also be used in the form UNLOCK ALL, which will release all locks in all work areas selected by the user.

The EDIT and CHANGE commands employ a manual method for locking and unlocking records. While the current record is being displayed on the screen by either of these commands, the user cannot make any changes unless the record is first locked by means of the CTRL and O key combination. The record may then be unlocked by means of the same key combination, or by moving on to another record.

The DISPLAY STATUS or LIST STATUS command provides an extra item of information when used with dBASE ADMINISTRATOR:

included amongst the information shown for each work area, it gives the current lock status. It indicates whether a file lock or a record lock is in operation and, if the latter, which record number is locked. The SET PRINTER TO command may also be used to obtain extra features. Printer output can be directed to a locally attached device or to a shared network printer.

There are a small number of other commands contained in dBASE ADMINISTRATOR but they rely on the special PROTECT utility program mentioned above. This utility provides the means of specifying a user log-on procedure complete with password, an access level for each user and each file so that a user's access level can be checked against the access level of a particular file, and data encryption for the data contained in the files. The associated features include the ACCESS( ) function which returns the user's access level as set by the PROTECT program, the LOGOUT command which forces a user log-out and prompts for a new user log-in, and the SET ENCRYPTION OFF command which allows you to specify that a new database file created by commands such as COPY or SORT should not be encrypted.

FoxBASE

FoxBASE is a fully compatible dBASE II look-alike that can be used with a network or with a multi-user minicomputer system. Running in the Unix/Xenix environment, the FoxBASE claims are that we can purchase a popular multi-user computer system such as that from Altos, and transfer our dBASE II applications lock stock and barrel into this multi-user environment. It meets its claim by incorporating an automatic record locking procedure that requires no modification of the original application, so that more than one user can use an application that was designed for a single user. FoxBASE also provides a number of new commands and functions that allow the dBASE programmer to lock database records and/or files to prevent simultaneous access by several users, particularly those trying to update the same record.

Before looking at these, let us examine a SET command that FoxBASE provides to let you deal with multiple access attempts. The SET LOCK TO command allows you to select one of four levels of locking. This command does not perform any locking itself, but determines the course of action to be taken when a user attempts to access a record that is already in use:

SET LOCK TO 0: The user will be asked to choose from one of four options, i.e. Wait, Retry, Ignore, or Escape. If the user elects to *Wait*, a

'Waiting ...' message is displayed until the record becomes available or the user ends the wait state. Selecting *Retry* will cause another attempt to lock the record, which will either succeed or return to the Wait, Retry, Ignore, or Escape set of options. Selecting *Ignore* will present the record, but any attempt to change the record contents will result in an error message. Selecting *Escape* will result in control leaving the application and being returned to the interpreter or Runtime system.

SET LOCK TO 1: This also relies on the user, but on an unsuccessful attempt to access a record it assumes that the user has selected the *Wait* option above, i.e. it displays the message 'Waiting ...' and proceeds as above.

SET LOCK TO 2: On an unsuccessful attempt to access a record, FoxBASE does not wait or consult the user but results in an error.

SET LOCK TO 3: This does not react to a multiple access. It expects the programmer to use the LOCK( ) and LOCKNDX( ) functions and the UNLOCK command to control multiple access. This level is also useful in situations where common access to a record may be for reading purposes only and there is thus no point in refusing multiple access.

The LOCK( ) function examines the current record and tries to lock it. If the function returns a logical True you have gained read and write access to the record and the LOCK( ) function will also have reread the record to provide the most recent possible copy of the record. If the function returns a logical False, it means that another user has gained write access. You may still use the record for read only purposes, but be aware that its contents may no longer be up to date since it may be in the process of being changed by another user. A locked record is automatically unlocked when the current record pointer is changed or if the database file is closed.

The LOCKNDX( ) function attempts to lock the database file currently in USE and thus all related indexes. The name is a misnomer, dating from a multi-user version of dBASE II itself and kept by Fox Software to maintain conformity. If the function returns a logical True, the lock has been successful. If it returns a logical False, it means that another user has locked the file. The file may be unlocked by the UNLOCK command, or it is automatically unlocked when the database file is closed.

The UNLOCK command removes all locks on the database file in the active work area.

Final word

There is more to using a multi-user system than meets the eye, and expressions like 'deadly embrace' and 'deadlock' have been coined to describe what happens if an application allows users to tie themselves into a knot. Typically these situations occur where one user has locked a record or file and is trying to lock a second record or file which a second user has already locked, while at the same time the second user is trying to lock the record or file already locked by the first user. If you add a recovery procedure which performs a continuous RETRY, you really have tied up the system and its users. It is important, therefore, to approach the locking procedure with some care. It is also important to test multi-user applications more thoroughly than you would single-user applications, since an error could bring down the system for all users, not just one.

Multi-user dBASE is in its infancy, and we may not yet have reached a standard approach that can properly be said to represent the dBASE language. Insofar as both of the two implementations discussed above employ record locking functions, we can view this as a language standard, but it remains to be seen what the other developments on this front produce. We must hope that the trend will be towards an approach which is in keeping with the dBASE philosophy of not involving the programmer in matters of technical detail.

Index